Smoker Cookbook

The Ultimate Cookbook for Smoking Meat, Complete Cookbook for Smoked Meat Lovers

By Dean Woods

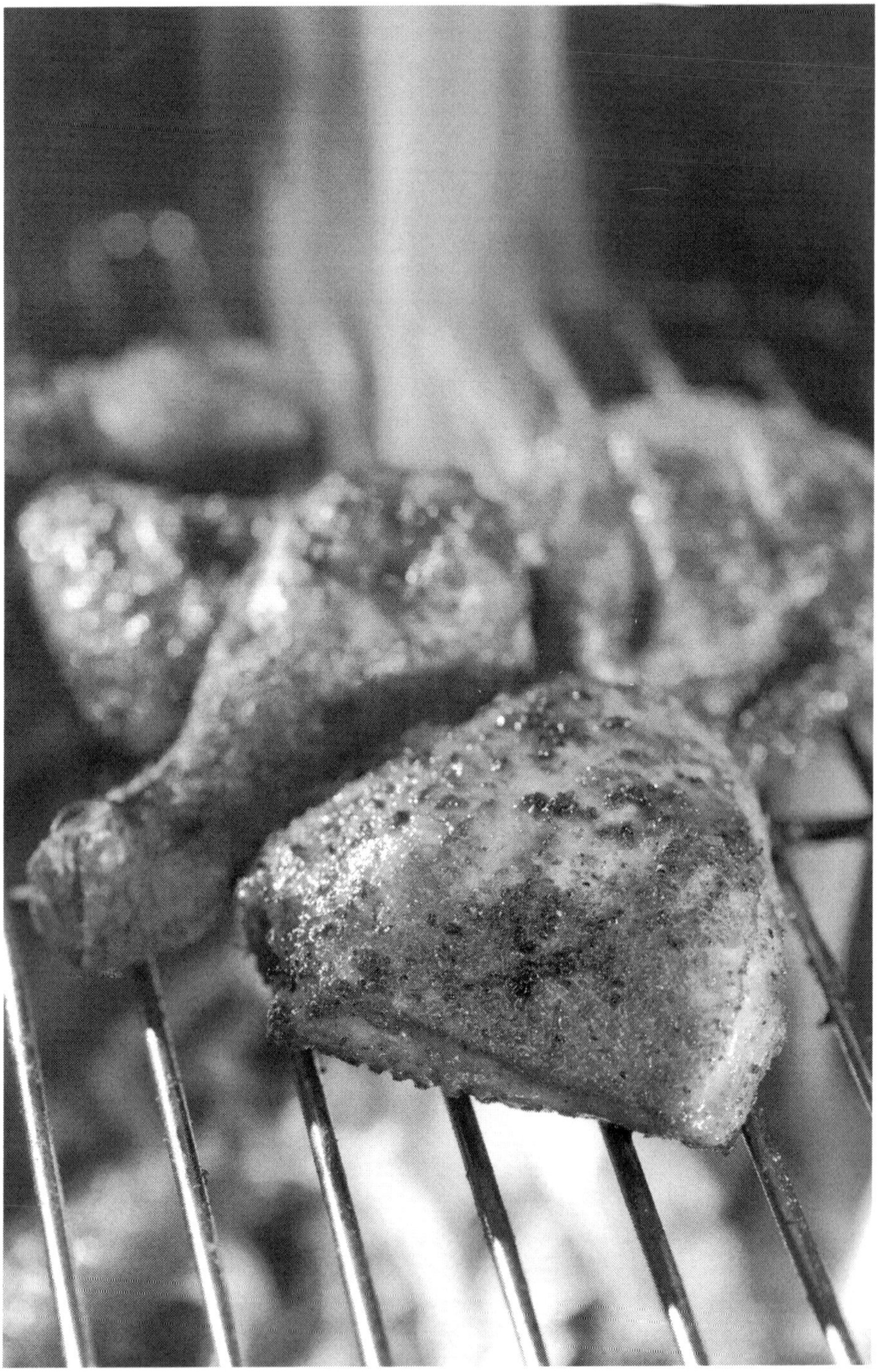

TABLE OF CONTENTS

INTRODUCTION 7

CHAPTER-1 BEEF RECIPES... 9
Beef Brisket.. 9
Beef Ribs 12
Pulled Beef Chuck Roast 15
Beef Roast.. 18
Beef Stew... 21

CHAPTER-2 PORK RECIPES 25
BBQ Pork Chops 25
Pork Shoulder with Cabbage Slaw 28
Glazed Spare Ribs... 32
Pork Steaks 35
Pork Butt Sandwiches 38

CHAPTER-3 LAMB RECIPES 42
Lamb Chops 42
Lamb Leg with Salsa Verde 45
Lamb Shoulder 48

Lamb Ribs 51

Lamb Breast 54

CHAPTER-4 CHICKEN RECIPES 57

Whole Chicken 57

Spicy Chicken Thighs 60

Maple Chipotle Chicken Breast 63

Chicken Wings 66

Chicken Halves 69

CHAPTER-5 TURKEY RECIPES 72

Whole Turkey 72

Turkey Breast 75

Turkey Legs 78

Turkey Wings 81

Bacon-Wrapped Turkey Breast 84

CHAPTER-6 FISH RECIPES 87

Brown Sugar Smoked Salmon 87

Smoked Trout Dip 90

Smoked Sardines 94

Caribbean Style Whole Red Snapper 97

CHAPTER-7 SEAFOOD RECIPES 100

Crab Legs..100

Garlic Prawns 103

Smoked Baby Octopus 106

Smoked Oysters 109

CHAPTER-8 GAME & RABBIT RECIPES 112

Smoked Duck 112

Smoked Pheasant..115

Citrus Goose Breast 118

Buffalo Chuck Roast 121

Bacon Wrapped Rabbit 124

CHAPTER-9 VEGETABLES & SNACK RECIPES............127

Smoke-Roasted Root Vegetables..127

Smoked Corn On The Cob 130

Smoked Artichokes 133

Smoked Tomatillo Salsa 136

Smoked Jalapeño Poppers..139

Beef Jerky 142

CHAPTER-10 SMOKING MEAT 145

SELECTING A SMOKER 145
CHOOSE YOUR WOOD 145
THE RIGHT TEMPERATURE 146
DIFFERENCE BETWEEN COLD AND HOT SMOKING 146
THE BASIC PREPARATIONS 147
THE CORE ELEMENTS OF SMOKING 148

CONCLUSION 149

MY BOOKS 150

Get Your FREE Gift 153

INTRODUCTION

Smoking is generally used as one of the cooking methods nowadays. The food enriches in protein such as meat would spoil quickly, if cooked for a longer period of time with modern cooking techniques. Whereas, Smoking is a low & slow process of cooking the meat. Where there is a smoke, there is a flavor. With white smoke, you can boost the flavor of your food. In addition to this statement, you can preserve the nutrition present in the food as well. This is flexible & one of the oldest techniques of making food. It's essential for you to brush the marinade over your food while you cook and let the miracle happen. The only thing you need to do is to add a handful of fresh coals or wood chips as and when required. Just taste your regular grilled meat and a smoked meat, you yourself would find the diffcrence. Remember one thing i.e. "Smoking is an art". With a little time & practice, even you can become an expert. Once you become an expert with smoking technique, believe me, you would never look for other cooking techniques. To find one which smoking technique works for you, you must experiment with different woods & cooking methods. Just cook the meat over indirect heat source & cook it for hours. When smoking your meats, it's very important that you let the smoke to escape & move around.

CHAPTER-1 BEEF RECIPES

Beef Brisket

TOTAL COOK TIME 7 HOURS

INGREDIENTS FOR 10 SERVINGS

- Beef brisket, fat trimmed – 6 pounds

THE RUB

- Onion powder – 3 tablespoons
- Garlic salt – 3 tablespoons
- Celery salt – 1 tablespoons
- Ground black pepper – 1 tablespoons
- White sugar – 3/4 cup
- Cayenne pepper – 1 teaspoon
- Paprika – 1 1/2 cups
- Dried thyme – 1/2 teaspoon
- Lemon pepper – 1 tablespoon
- Mustard powder – 1 teaspoon

THE FIRE

- Firstly, let soak 7 cups of wood chips, any flavor, in warm water for 30 minutes and then make packets of soaked woodchips, 1 cup per packet, by wrapping them in an aluminum foil.
- Arrange unlit charcoals on one side of charcoal grate into the smoker, then top with hot charcoals.
- Place a drip pan on the other side of smoker, 3/4 full with water and set smoking grate in place.
- Set the lid and wait until the temperature reached 225 degrees through temperature gauge or temperature probes while keeping more hot coals prepare.

Method

- Before setting smoker, let beef brisket marinate.
- For this, stir together all the ingredients for rub until combined and then rub this mixture generously all over the meat.
- Then place brisket in the refrigerator and let marinate overnight.
- When ready to smoke, place a prepared pouch of woodchips over charcoal and when start to smoke, brush the smoking grate with oil generously, place seasoned brisket on the grate above the drip pan and insert thermometer probe in the thickest part of the meat.
- Set lid on smoker and monitor temperature through temperature gauge or temperature probes and maintain it.
- Close down the lower air vent if the temperature is above 250 degrees or open up the lower air vent if the temperature drops below 255 degrees F and add few more hot coals.
- Check every hour if more water needs to add in the drip pan and add more hot coals using tongs along with another pouch of wood chips to keep the smoke going.
- Let smoke for 7 hours, flip halfway through, until meat is cooked through and inserted meat thermometer register 185 degrees F temperature.
- When done, let beef brisket rest for 10 minutes and then slice to serve.

Beef Ribs

TOTAL COOK TIME 4 HOURS

Ingredients for 6 servings

- Rack of beef ribs, membrane removed – 2

THE RUB

- Onion powder – 1 tablespoon
- Garlic powder – 1 tablespoon
- Salt – 1 tablespoon
- Ground black pepper – 1 tablespoon
- Brown sugar – 1/4 cup
- Red chili powder – 1 tablespoon
- Cayenne pepper – 1/2 teaspoon
- Cumin – 2 teaspoon
- Ground coriander – 2 teaspoon
- Dried oregano – 2 teaspoon
- Dried thyme – 1/4 teaspoon

THE FIRE

- Firstly, let soak 4 cups of wood chips, any flavor, in warm water for 30 minutes and then make packets of soaked woodchips, 1 cup per packet, by wrapping them in an aluminum foil.
- Arrange unlit charcoals on one side of charcoal grate into the smoker, then top with hot charcoals.
- Place a drip pan on the other side of smoker, 3/4 full with water and set smoking grate in place.
- Set the lid and wait until the temperature reached 225 degrees through temperature gauge or temperature probes while keeping more hot coals prepare.

Method

- In the meantime, season beef ribs.

- For this, stir together all the ingredients for rub until combined and then rub this mixture generously all over the rack of ribs.

- When ready to smoke, place a prepared pouch of woodchips over charcoal and when start to smoke, brush the smoking grate with oil generously, place ribs on the grate above the drip pan and insert thermometer probe in the thickest part of the meat.

- Set lid on smoker and monitor temperature through temperature gauge or temperature probes and maintain it.

- Close down the lower air vent if the temperature is above 250 degrees or open up the lower air vent if the temperature drops below 255 degrees F and add few more hot coals.

- Check every hour if more water needs to add in the drip pan and add more hot coals using tongs along with another pouch of wood chips to keep the smoke going.

- Let smoke for 4 hours or until ribs bend and meat is very tender and inserted meat thermometer register 190 to 200 degrees F temperature.

- Slice and serve.

Pulled Beef Chuck Roast

TOTAL COOK TIME 9 HOURS

INGREDIENTS FOR 6 SERVINGS

- Chuck roast, fat trimmed – 4 pounds

The Rub

- Salt – 2 tablespoons
- Ground black pepper – 2 tablespoons
- Garlic powder – 2 tablespoons

The Rub

- White onion, peeled and sliced – 1
- Beef stock, divided – 3 cups

The Fire

- Firstly, let soak 9 cups of wood chips, any flavor, in warm water for 30 minutes and then make packets of soaked woodchips, 1 cup per packet, by wrapping them in an aluminum foil.
- Arrange unlit charcoals on one side of charcoal grate into the smoker, then top with hot charcoals.
- Place a drip pan on the other side of smoker, 3/4 full with water and set smoking grate in place.
- Set the lid and wait until the temperature reached 225 degrees through temperature gauge or temperature probes while keeping more hot coals prepare.

Method

- Before setting smoker, let beef marinate.
- For this, stir together all the ingredients for rub until combined and then rub this mixture generously all over the meat.
- Then place brisket in the refrigerator and let marinate overnight.

- When ready to smoke, place a prepared pouch of woodchips over charcoal and when start to smoke, brush the smoking grate with oil generously, place seasoned brisket on the grate above the drip pan and insert thermometer probe in the thickest part of the meat.

- Set lid on smoker and monitor temperature through temperature gauge or temperature probes and maintain it.

- Close down the lower air vent if the temperature is above 250 degrees or open up the lower air vent if the temperature drops below 255 degrees F and add few more hot coals.

- Check every hour if more water needs to add in the drip pan and add more hot coals using tongs along with another pouch of wood chips to keep the smoke going.

- Let smoke for 3 hours and spray meat with 1 cup of beef stock every hour.

- After 3 hours, scatter slices of onion in the bottom of the large aluminum pan, pour beef stock evenly and transfer smoked beef roast in it.

- Place pan into the smoker and continue smoking for 3 hours or until inserted meat thermometer register 165 degrees F temperature.

- Now, cover pan tightly with aluminum foil and continue smoking for another 3 hours or until inserted meat thermometer register 200 degrees F temperature.

- Remove roast from the smoker and let rest for 15 minutes.

- Transfer roast from pan to a plate and shred using forks.

- Separate fats from the cooking liquid and add it to the shred meat until moisten.

- Serve as a sandwich.

Beef Roast

TOTAL COOK TIME 5 HOURS

INGREDIENTS FOR 6 SERVINGS

- Beef roast – 3 pounds

THE RUB

- Salt – 1 ½ teaspoon
- Ground black pepper – 1 teaspoon
- Garlic powder – 1 teaspoon
- Smoked paprika – 1 teaspoon
- Onion powder – ½ teaspoon
- Worcestershire sauce – ½ cup

THE FIRE

- Firstly, let soak 5 cups of wood chips, any flavor, in warm water for 30 minutes and then make packets of soaked woodchips, 1 cup per packet, by wrapping them in an aluminum foil.
- Arrange unlit charcoals on one side of charcoal grate into the smoker, then top with hot charcoals.
- Place a drip pan on the other side of smoker, 3/4 full with water and set smoking grate in place.
- Set the lid and wait until the temperature reached 225 degrees through temperature gauge or temperature probes while keeping more hot coals prepare.

METHOD

- In the meantime, season beef roast.
- For this, place all the ingredients for the rub, except for Worcestershire sauce, in a bowl and stir until mixed.
- Brush beef roast with Worcestershire sauce and then sprinkle with prepared rub.
- When ready to smoke, place a prepared pouch of woodchips over charcoal and when start to smoke, brush the smoking grate with oil generously, place seasoned beef roast on the grate above the drip pan and insert thermometer probe in the thickest part of the meat.
- Set lid on smoker and monitor temperature through temperature gauge or temperature probes and maintain it.
- Close down the lower air vent if the temperature is above 250 degrees or open up the lower air vent if the temperature drops below 255 degrees F and add few more hot coals.
- Check every hour if more water needs to add in the drip pan and add more hot coals using tongs along with another pouch of wood chips to keep the smoke going.
- Let smoke for 5 to 6 hours or until meat is cooked through and inserted meat thermometer register 145 to 150 degrees F temperature.
- When done, remove roast from the smoker, then wrap tightly with aluminum foil and let rest for 20 minutes.
- Then slice roast and serve.

Beef Stew

TOTAL COOK TIME **6** HOURS

INGREDIENTS FOR **6** SERVINGS

- Beef stew meat, cubed – 2 pounds

The Rub

- Garlic powder – 1 teaspoon
- Salt – 1 teaspoon
- Ground black pepper – 1 teaspoon
- White sugar – 1 tablespoon
- Cayenne pepper – 1/2 teaspoon
- Paprika – 1 tablespoon
- Dried oregano – 2 teaspoons
- Dried thyme – 1/2 teaspoon

Other Ingredients

- Medium white onions, peeled and diced – 2
- Medium carrots, peeled and diced – 6
- Medium potatoes, peeled and diced – 6
- Diced tomatoes – 28 ounce
- Cornstarch – 1 tablespoon
- Water – 1 tablespoon
- Beef broth – 5 cups

THE FIRE

- Firstly, let soak 2 cups of wood chips, any flavor, in warm water for 30 minutes and then make packets of soaked woodchips, 1 cup per packet, by wrapping them in an aluminum foil.

- Arrange unlit charcoals on one side of charcoal grate into the smoker, then top with hot charcoals.

- Place a drip pan on the other side of smoker, 3/4 full with water and set smoking grate in place.

- Set the lid and wait until the temperature reached 225 degrees through temperature gauge or temperature probes while keeping more hot coals prepare.

METHOD

- In the meantime, stir together ingredients for the rub in a bowl until combined.

- Rub this rub generously all over the meat pieces and then place in an aluminum pan.

- When ready to smoke, place a prepared pouch of woodchips over charcoal and when start to smoke, place aluminum pan containing meat on the grate above the drip pan.

- Set lid on smoker and monitor temperature through temperature gauge or temperature probes and maintain it.

- Close down the lower air vent if the temperature is above 250 degrees or open up the lower air vent if the temperature drops below 255 degrees F and add few more hot coals.

- Check every hour if more water needs to add in the drip pan and add more hot coals using tongs along with another pouch of wood chips to keep the smoke going.

- Let smoke for 2 hours and when done, transfer meat to a 6-quart slow cooker.
- Add onion, carrots, potatoes, and tomatoes into the slow cooker and pour in beef broth.
- Cover with its lid, plug in the slow cooker and let cook for 4 hours at high heat setting.
- When 15 minutes are left, stir in cornstarch and water mixture and continue cooking or until cooking liquid is slightly thick.
- Serve stew with bread.

CHAPTER-2 PORK RECIPES

BBQ Pork Chops

TOTAL COOK TIME 1 HOUR

INGREDIENTS FOR 4 SERVINGS

- Pork Chops, center-cut – 4

The Rub

- Onion powder – 2 tablespoons
- Salt – 4 tablespoon
- Ground black pepper – 2 tablespoons
- Brown sugar – 2 tablespoons
- Cayenne pepper – 1 tablespoon
- Ground thyme – 2 tablespoons

The Sauce

- Brown sugar – 1 tablespoon
- Apple cider – 1 cup
- BBQ sauce – 1/2 cup
- Buttermilk – 1 tablespoon

The Fire

- Firstly, let soak 2 cups of wood chips, any flavor, in warm water for 30 minutes and then make a packet of soaked woodchips by wrapping them in an aluminum foil.

- Arrange unlit charcoals on one side of charcoal grate into the smoker, then top with hot charcoals.

- Place a drip pan on the other side of smoker, 3/4 full with water and set smoking grate in place.

- Set the lid and wait until the temperature reached 275 degrees through temperature gauge or temperature probes while keeping more hot coals prepare.

METHOD

- Before setting smoker, let pork chops marinate.

- For this, stir together ingredients for rub and rub all over the pork chops.

- Place pork chops in a re-sealable bag, seal it and let marinate in the refrigerator for 4 hours or overnight.

- When ready to smoke, place a prepared pouch of woodchips over charcoal and when start to smoke, brush the smoking grate with oil generously, place marinated pork chops on the grate above the drip pan and insert thermometer probe in the thickest part of the meat.

- Set lid on smoker and monitor temperature through temperature gauge or temperature probes and maintain it.

- Close down the lower air vent if the temperature is above 270 degrees or open up the lower air vent if the temperature drops below 250 degrees F and add few more hot coals.

- Let smoke for 1 hour or until meat is cooked through and firm.

- In the meantime, prepare butter barbecue sauce.

- Place a saucepan over medium-low heat, pour in apple cider and stir in sugar until combined.

- Let cook for 25 minutes or until sauce is reduced by half.

- Lower to heat to a low level, whisk in BBQ sauce until mixed well and let cook until warm through.

- Then remove the pan from heat and whisk in buttermilk until incorporated.

- Drizzle this sauce over smoked pork chops and serve.

Pork Shoulder with Cabbage Slaw

TOTAL COOK TIME 5 HOURS

Ingredients for 10 servings

- Pork shoulder, boneless and fat trimmed – 5 pounds

The Marinate

- Large white onion, peeled and chopped – 1
- Chipotle in adobo, chopped – 2
- Minced garlic – 1 tablespoon

- Brown sugar – 2 tablespoons
- Ancho Chile powder – 2 tablespoons
- Ground cumin – 2 teaspoons
- Dried thyme – ½ teaspoon
- Ground coriander – 1 teaspoon
- Olive oil – 2 tablespoons
- Lime juice – 1/2 cup
- Orange juice – 3/4 cup
- Water – ½ cup

THE SLAW

- Head of napa cabbage, shredded – 1
- Large carrot, peeled and julienned – 1
- Green onions, chopped – 4
- Serrano chiles – 2
- Celery seeds – 1 teaspoon
- Salt – ¾ teaspoon
- Ground black pepper – ½ teaspoon
- Apple cider vinegar – 1/4 cup
- Olive oil – 2 tablespoons
- Mayonnaise – 1/4 cup
- Queso fresco crumbled – 1/2 cup

The Fire

- Firstly, let soak 5 cups of wood chips, any flavor, in warm water for 30 minutes and then make packets of soaked woodchips, 1 cup per packet, by wrapping them in an aluminum foil.

- Arrange unlit charcoals on one side of charcoal grate into the smoker, then top with hot charcoals.

- Place a drip pan on the other side of smoker, 3/4 full with water and set smoking grate in place.

- Set the lid and wait until the temperature reached 225 degrees through temperature gauge or temperature probes while keeping more hot coals prepare.

Method

- Before setting smoker, let the pork marinate.

- For this, place a saucepan over medium heat, add oil and when heated, add remaining ingredients for the marinade.

- Let cook for 5 to 7 minutes or until sugar dissolves completely.

- Then remove the pan from heat and let marinade cool.

- Place pork shoulder in a large pan, pour over prepared marinade, then cover pan and let marinate overnight in the refrigerator.

- Remove pork from refrigerator 30 minutes before smoking.

- When ready to smoke, place a prepared pouch of woodchips over charcoal and when to start to smoke, brush the smoking grate with oil generously, place pork shoulder on the grate above the drip pan and insert thermometer probe in the thickest part of the meat.

- Set lid on smoker and monitor temperature through temperature gauge or temperature probes and maintain it.

- Close down the lower air vent if the temperature is above 250 degrees or open up the lower air vent if the temperature drops below 255 degrees F and add few more hot coals.

- Check every hour if more water needs to add in the drip pan and add more hot coals using tongs along with another pouch of wood chips to keep the smoke going.

- Let smoke for 5 hours or until meat is cooked through and inserted meat thermometer register 140 degrees F temperature.

- Then remove pork from smoker and let rest for 30 minutes.

- In the meantime, prepare cabbage slaw.

- Place mayonnaise in a bowl and whisk in celery seed, salt, black pepper, vinegar and oil until combined.

- Stir in green onion and chilies.

- Place cabbage and carrot in a bowl, pour over prepared mayonnaise dressing along with queso fresco and toss to combine.

- Shred pork shoulder and serve with tortilla and cabbage slaw.

Glazed Spare Ribs

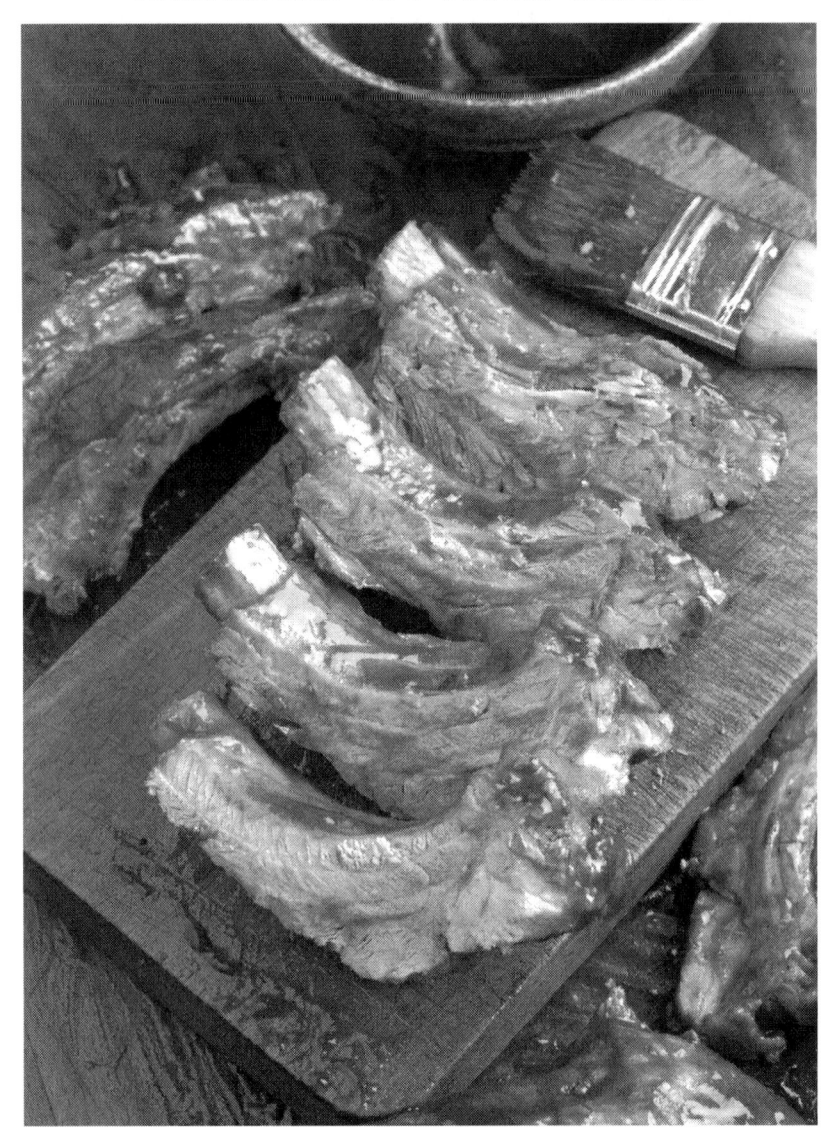

TOTAL COOK TIME 4 HOURS AND 30 MINUTES

INGREDIENTS FOR 6 SERVINGS

- Pork spare ribs – 3 pounds

THE RUB

- Onion powder – 1 teaspoon
- Garlic powder – 1 teaspoon
- Salt – 2 teaspoons
- Lemon pepper – 1 teaspoon
- Roasted garlic pepper seasoning – 1 tablespoon

THE GLAZE

- Honey – 1/2 cup
- Brown sugar – 1/2 cup

THE FIRE

- Firstly, let soak 5 cups of wood chips, any flavor, in warm water for 30 minutes and then make packets of soaked woodchips, 1 cup per packet, by wrapping them in an aluminum foil.
- Arrange unlit charcoals on one side of charcoal grate into the smoker, then top with hot charcoals.
- Place a drip pan on the other side of smoker, 3/4 full with water and set smoking grate in place.
- Set the lid and wait until the temperature reached 225 degrees through temperature gauge or temperature probes while keeping more hot coals prepare.

METHOD

- In the meantime, seasoned spare ribs.

- For this, stir together all the ingredients for rub and rub generously all over the pork ribs.

- When ready to smoke, place a prepared pouch of woodchips over charcoal and when start to smoke, brush the smoking grate with oil generously, place seasoned pork ribs on the grate above the drip pan and insert thermometer probe in the thickest part of the meat.

- Set lid on smoker and monitor temperature through temperature gauge or temperature probes and maintain it.

- Close down the lower air vent if the temperature is above 250 degrees or open up the lower air vent if the temperature drops below 255 degrees F and add few more hot coals.

- Check every hour if more water needs to add in the drip pan and add more hot coals using tongs along with another pouch of wood chips to keep the smoke going.

- Let smoke for 4 hours or until meat is cooked through and inserted meat thermometer register 150 to 165 degrees F temperature.

- Whisk together honey and sugar and then brush over pork ribs.

- Continue smoking for 30 minutes.

- Slice and serve.

Pork Steaks

TOTAL COOK TIME **6** HOURS

INGREDIENTS FOR **12** SERVINGS

- Pork butt – 6 pounds

THE RUB

- Chinese five-spice powder – 2 tablespoons
- Brown sugar – 1 1/2 tablespoons
- Salt – 1 1/2 tablespoons

THE SAUCE

- Chinese five-spice powder – 2 teaspoons

- Honey – 1/2 cup
- Soy sauce – 1/2 cup
- Hoisin sauce – 2/3 cup
- Dry sherry – 1/3 cup

THE FIRE

- Firstly, let soak 6 cups of wood chips, any flavor, in warm water for 30 minutes and then make packets of soaked woodchips, 1 cup per packet, by wrapping them in an aluminum foil.
- Arrange unlit charcoals on one side of charcoal grate into the smoker, then top with hot charcoals.
- Place a drip pan on the other side of smoker, 3/4 full with water and set smoking grate in place.
- Set the lid and wait until the temperature reached 225 degrees through temperature gauge or temperature probes while keeping more hot coals prepare.

METHOD

- Before setting smoker, let the pork marinate.
- For this, slice pork into 2-inch thick steaks.
- Whisk together ingredients for rub until combined, then rub generously all over pork steaks and place in a large resealable plastic bag.
- Whisk together ingredients of sauce until well combined and add to pork.
- Seal the bag, turn it upside down until pork steaks are coated and then let marinate overnight in the refrigerator.

- When ready to smoke, place a prepared pouch of woodchips over charcoal and when start to smoke, brush the smoking grate with oil generously.

- Remove pork chops from marinade and place them on the grate above the drip pan and insert thermometer probe in the thickest part of the meat, reserve the marinade.

- Set lid on smoker and monitor temperature through temperature gauge or temperature probes and maintain it.

- Close down the lower air vent if the temperature is above 250 degrees or open up the lower air vent if the temperature drops below 255 degrees F and add few more hot coals.

- Check every hour if more water needs to add in the drip pan and add more hot coals using tongs along with another pouch of wood chips to keep the smoke going.

- Let smoke for 5 hours and 30 minutes or until meat is cooked through and inserted meat thermometer register 150 to 165 degrees F temperature.

- In the meantime, place reserved marinade in a small saucepan, place pan over medium heat and bring to boil.

- Then reduce heat to low and simmer sauce for 10 minutes or until reduced by half.

- Then remove saucepan from heat and brush it all overcooked pork steaks.

- Return steaks to the smoker and continue smoking for another 30 minutes.

- When done, let pork steaks rest for 15 minutes and then serve.

Pork Butt Sandwiches

TOTAL COOK TIME 7 HOURS AND 30 MINUTES

INGREDIENTS FOR 8 SERVINGS

- Pork Butt – 5 pounds

THE RUB

- Celery seeds – 1/2 teaspoon
- Garlic powder – 1 teaspoon
- Salt – 1 tablespoon
- Ground black pepper – 1 teaspoon
- Brown sugar – 2 tablespoons
- Red chili powder – 1 teaspoon
- Cayenne pepper – 1 teaspoon
- Paprika – 2 teaspoons
- Dry mustard powder – 1 tablespoon

THE SLAW

- Carrots, peeled and grated – 2
- Green cabbage, sliced into ribbons – 1 1/2 pound
- Grated shallot – 2 tablespoons
- Celery seeds – 1 teaspoon
- Salt – 1 teaspoon
- Ground black pepper – 1 teaspoon
- White sugar – 2 tablespoons
- Yellow mustard – 1 tablespoon
- Apple cider vinegar – 6 tablespoons
- Olive oil – 2 tablespoons

- Mayonnaise – 1 tablespoon

OTHER INGREDIENTS

- Burger buns, halved and toasted – for serving

THE FIRE

- Firstly, let soak 8 cups of wood chips, any flavor, in warm water for 30 minutes and then make packets of soaked woodchips, 1 cup per packet, by wrapping them in an aluminum foil.
- Arrange unlit charcoals on one side of charcoal grate into the smoker, then top with hot charcoals.
- Place a drip pan on the other side of smoker, 3/4 full with water and set smoking grate in place.
- Set the lid and wait until the temperature reached 275 degrees through temperature gauge or temperature probes while keeping more hot coals prepare.

METHOD

- Before setting smoker, let the pork marinate.
- For this, stir together all the ingredients for rub and rub all over the pork generously.
- Place seasoned pork on a rimmed tray, cover with plastic wrap and let marinate for 1 hour at room temperature.
- When ready to smoke, place a prepared pouch of woodchips over charcoal and when to start to smoke, brush the smoking grate with oil generously, place pork on the grate above the drip pan and insert thermometer probe in the thickest part of the meat.

- Set lid on smoker and monitor temperature through temperature gauge or temperature probes and maintain it.

- Close down the lower air vent if the temperature is above 300 degrees or open up the lower air vent if the temperature drops below 275 degrees F and add few more hot coals.

- Check every hour if more water needs to add in the drip pan and add more hot coals using tongs along with another pouch of wood chips to keep the smoke going.

- Let smoke for 7 hours and 30 minutes or until meat is cooked through and inserted meat thermometer register 190 degrees F temperature.

- In the meantime, prepare the slaw.

- First, whisk together celery seeds, salt, black pepper, sugar, mustard, oil, vinegar, and mayonnaise in a large bowl until well combined.

- Add shallots, cabbage, and carrots and toss to coat.

- Cover bowl with plastic wrap and let chill in refrigerator until required.

- When pork is smoked, remove from smoker and let rest for 30 minutes before shredding with forks.

- Roast buns, top with shredded pork and prepared slaw and serve.

CHAPTER-3 LAMB RECIPES

Lamb Chops

TOTAL COOK TIME 2 HOURS AND 10 MINUTES

INGREDIENTS FOR 4 SERVINGS

- Rack of lamb chops, sliced – 1

The Marinate

- Salt – 1 teaspoon
- Ground Pepper – 2 teaspoons
- Apple cider vinegar – 2 teaspoons

The Fire

- Firstly, let soak 2 cups of wood chips, any flavor, in warm water for 30 minutes and then make packets of soaked woodchips, 1 cup per packet, by wrapping them in an aluminum foil.
- Arrange unlit charcoals on one side of charcoal grate into the smoker, then top with hot charcoals.
- Place a drip pan on the other side of smoker, 3/4 full with water and set smoking grate in place.
- Set the lid and wait until the temperature reached 225 degrees through temperature gauge or temperature probes while keeping more hot coals prepare.

Method

- In the meantime, place all the ingredients for marinade in a large bowl and stir until mixed.

- Add lamb chops and toss to coat.

- When ready to smoke, place a prepared pouch of woodchips over charcoal and when start to smoke, brush the smoking grate with oil generously, place lamb chops on the grate above the drip pan and insert thermometer probe in the thickest part of the meat.

- Set lid on smoker and monitor temperature through temperature gauge or temperature probes and maintain it.

- Close down the lower air vent if the temperature is above 250 degrees or open up the lower air vent if the temperature drops below 255 degrees F and add few more hot coals.

- Check every hour if more water needs to add in the drip pan and add more hot coals using tongs along with another pouch of wood chips to keep the smoke going.

- Let smoke for 2 hours or until chops are cooked to desired doneness and inserted meat thermometer register 145 degrees F temperature.

- When done, place a griddle pan over medium-high heat, grease with oil and place lamb chops in it.

- Let grill for 5 minutes per side and then serve with a salad.

Lamb Leg with Salsa Verde

TOTAL COOK TIME 5 HOURS

Ingredients for 8 servings

- Leg of lamb, fat trimmed – 6 pounds

The Rub

- Garlic head, peeled – 1
- Salt – 2 tablespoons
- Chopped rosemary – 2 tablespoons

- Ground black pepper – 1 teaspoon
- Beef broth – ¼ cup

The Salsa

- Dill pickle cucumbers, chopped – 3 ounce
- Anchovies, chopped – 8
- Minced garlic – 1 teaspoon
- Parsley, chopped – ½ cup
- Basil, chopped – ½ cup
- Salt – ½ teaspoon
- Ground black pepper – ¼ teaspoon
- Honey – 1 teaspoon
- Olive oil – ¾ cup

The Fire

- Firstly, let soak 5 cups of wood chips, any flavor, in warm water for 30 minutes and then make packets of soaked woodchips, 1 cup per packet, by wrapping them in an aluminum foil.
- Arrange unlit charcoals on one side of charcoal grate into the smoker, then top with hot charcoals.
- Place a drip pan on the other side of smoker, 3/4 full with water and set smoking grate in place.
- Set the lid and wait until the temperature reached 225 degrees through temperature gauge or temperature probes while keeping more hot coals prepare.

METHOD

- Before setting smoker, let leg of lamb marinate.

- For this, make deep cuts all the over the meat of lamb and stuff garlic cloves in it.

- Then season with salt, black pepper, and rosemary and let marinate for 30 minutes at room temperature.

- When ready to smoke, place a prepared pouch of woodchips over charcoal and when start to smoke, brush the smoking grate with oil generously, place leg of lamb on the grate above the drip pan and insert thermometer probe in the thickest part of the meat.

- Set lid on smoker and monitor temperature through temperature gauge or temperature probes and maintain it.

- Close down the lower air vent if the temperature is above 250 degrees or open up the lower air vent if the temperature drops below 255 degrees F and add few more hot coals.

- Check every hour if more water needs to add in the drip pan and add more hot coals using tongs along with another pouch of wood chips to keep the smoke going.

- Let smoke for 5 hours or until meat is cooked through and inserted meat thermometer register 150 degrees F temperature.

- In the meantime, prepare salsa verde.

- For this, place all the ingredients for salsa in a bowl and mix until well combined.

- Serve leg of lamb with salsa.

Lamb Shoulder

TOTAL COOK TIME **6** HOURS

Ingredients for **8** servings

- Lamb shoulder, fat trimmed – 5 pounds
- Apple cider vinegar – 1 cup

The Rub

- Salt – 2 tablespoons
- Ground black pepper – 2 tablespoons
- Dried rosemary – 1 tablespoon
- Olive oil – ½ cup

The Spritz

- Apple juice – 1 cup
- Apple cider vinegar – 1 cup

The Fire

- Firstly, let soak 6 cups of wood chips, any flavor, in warm water for 30 minutes and then make packets of soaked woodchips, 1 cup per packet, by wrapping them in an aluminum foil.
- Arrange unlit charcoals on one side of charcoal grate into the smoker, then top with hot charcoals.
- Place a drip pan on the other side of smoker, 3/4 full with water and set smoking grate in place.
- Set the lid and wait until the temperature reached 225 degrees through temperature gauge or temperature probes while keeping more hot coals prepare.

METHOD

- In the meantime, season lamb.
- For this, rinse lamb, pat dry and then inject with apple cider vinegar.
- Whisk together ingredients for the rub, then brush generously all over lamb and tie lamb with kitchen twine tightly.
- When ready to smoke, place a prepared pouch of woodchips over charcoal and when start to smoke, brush the smoking grate with oil generously, place lamb on the grate above the drip pan and insert thermometer probe in the thickest part of the meat.
- Let smoker for 1 hour, smoker uncovered and smoker uncovered and spritzing with the mixture of apple juice and vinegar using a spray bottle.
- Then set the lid on the smoker and continue smoking for 3 hours or until inserted meat thermometer register 165 degrees F.
- Monitor temperature through temperature gauge or temperature probes and maintain it.
- Close down the lower air vent if the temperature is above 250 degrees or open up the lower air vent if the temperature drops below 255 degrees F and add few more hot coals.
- Check every hour if more water needs to add in the drip pan and add more hot coals using tongs along with another pouch of wood chips to keep the smoke going.
- After 3 hours, wrap lamb with aluminum foil and continue smoking for 2 hours or until meat is very tender.
- When done, remove lamb from smoker and let rest for 1 hour.
- Shred lamb and serve.

Lamb Ribs

TOTAL COOK TIME 3 HOURS

INGREDIENTS FOR 4 SERVINGS

- Lamb ribs, membrane removed – 3 pounds

The Rub

- Paprika – 2 tablespoons
- Brown sugar – 1 tablespoon
- Ground mustard – 1 tablespoon
- Garlic powder – 2 teaspoons
- Dried thyme – 2 teaspoons
- Lemon pepper seasoning – 1 teaspoon
- Ground rosemary – 1 teaspoon
- Ground coriander – 1/2 teaspoon

Other Ingredients

- Salt – ¾ teaspoon
- Mayonnaise – ¼ cup

The Fire

- Firstly, let soak 2 cups of wood chips, any flavor, in warm water for 30 minutes and then make packets of soaked woodchips, 1 cup per packet, by wrapping them in an aluminum foil.
- Arrange unlit charcoals on one side of charcoal grate into the smoker, then top with hot charcoals.
- Place a drip pan on the other side of smoker, 3/4 full with water and set smoking grate in place.
- Set the lid and wait until the temperature reached 225 degrees through temperature gauge or temperature probes while keeping more hot coals prepare.

METHOD

- Before setting smoker, let season lamb ribs.
- Season lamb ribs with salt and then let rest for 2 hours at room temperature.
- Stir together ingredients for rub and set aside until required.
- When ready to smoke, place a prepared pouch of woodchips over charcoal and when start to smoke, brush the smoking grate with oil generously.
- Brush mayonnaise all over the ribs, then season with prepared rub, place them on the grate above the drip pan and insert thermometer probe in the thickest part of the meat.
- Set lid on smoker and monitor temperature through temperature gauge or temperature probes and maintain it.
- Close down the lower air vent if the temperature is above 250 degrees or open up the lower air vent if the temperature drops below 255 degrees F and add few more hot coals.
- Check every hour if more water needs to add in the drip pan and add more hot coals using tongs along with another pouch of wood chips to keep the smoke going.
- Let smoke for 4 hours or until ribs bend and meat is very tender.
- Slice to serve.

Lamb Breast

TOTAL COOK TIME 2 HOURS AND 30 MINUTES

INGREDIENTS FOR 2 SERVINGS

- Lamb breast, fat trimmed – 2 pounds

The Rub

- Onion powder – 1 teaspoon
- Garlic powder – 1 teaspoon
- Salt – 1 ½ tablespoon
- Ground black pepper – 1 tablespoon
- Brown sugar – 3 tablespoons
- Red chili powder – 1 tablespoon
- Paprika – 3 tablespoons

Other Ingredients

- Apple cider vinegar – ½ cup
- Mustard paste – ¼ cup

The Fire

- Firstly, let soak 3 cups of wood chips, any flavor, in warm water for 30 minutes and then make packets of soaked woodchips, 1 cup per packet, by wrapping them in an aluminum foil.

- Arrange unlit charcoals on one side of charcoal grate into the smoker, then top with hot charcoals.

- Place a drip pan on the other side of smoker, 3/4 full with water and set smoking grate in place.

- Set the lid and wait until the temperature reached 225 degrees through temperature gauge or temperature probes while keeping more hot coals prepare.

Method

- In the meantime, season lamb breasts.

- For this stir together ingredients for spice rub and generously rub all over the breast.

- When ready to smoke, place a prepared pouch of woodchips over charcoal and when start to smoke, brush the smoking grate with oil generously, place lamb breast on the grate above the drip pan and insert thermometer probe in the thickest part of the meat.

- Set lid on smoker and monitor temperature through temperature gauge or temperature probes and maintain it.

- Close down the lower air vent if the temperature is above 250 degrees or open up the lower air vent if the temperature drops below 255 degrees F and add few more hot coals.

- Check every hour if more water needs to add in the drip pan and add more hot coals using tongs along with another pouch of wood chips to keep the smoke going.

- Let smoke for 2 to 2 hours and 30 minutes or until meat is cooked through and inserted meat thermometer register 165 degrees F temperature.

- When done, remove lamb breast from the oven and let rest for 10 minutes.

- Slice and serve with salad.

CHAPTER-4 CHICKEN RECIPES

Whole Chicken

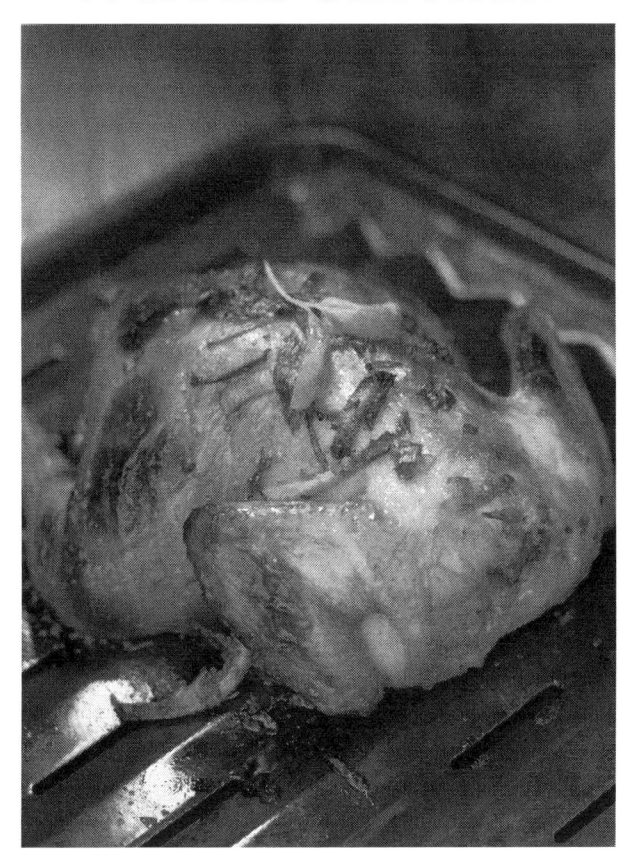

TOTAL COOK TIME 2 HOURS AND 30 MINUTES

INGREDIENTS FOR 6 SERVINGS

- Whole chicken – 3 pounds

The Rub

- Minced garlic – 1 teaspoon
- Medium white onion, peeled and sliced – 1
- Cloves of garlic, peeled – 3
- Sprigs of thyme – 4
- Lemon, sliced – 1

The Brine

- Salt – 1/4 cup
- Brown sugar – 1 cup
- Water – 1 gallon

The Fire

- Firstly, let soak 3 cups of wood chips, any flavor, in warm water for 30 minutes and then make packets of soaked woodchips, 1 cup per packet, by wrapping them in an aluminum foil.
- Arrange unlit charcoals on one side of charcoal grate into the smoker, then top with hot charcoals.
- Place a drip pan on the other side of smoker, 3/4 full with water and set smoking grate in place.
- Set the lid and wait until the temperature reached 225 degrees through temperature gauge or temperature probes while keeping more hot coals prepare.

Method

- Before setting smoker, let the chicken soak in brine.
- For this, pour in brine in a large container and stir in salt and sugar until dissolved.
- Then add chicken and let soak overnight in the refrigerator.
- Stir together ingredients for rub and set aside when required.
- Remove chicken from brine, rinse thoroughly, then pat dry and rub generously with garlic and prepared rub.
- Stuff cavity of chicken with onion, garlic, lemon and thyme and then tie its legs.
- When ready to smoke, place a prepared pouch of woodchips over charcoal and when to start to smoke, brush the smoking grate with oil generously, place chicken on the grate above the drip pan and insert thermometer probe in the thickest part of the meat.
- Set lid on smoker and monitor temperature through temperature gauge or temperature probes and maintain it.
- Close down the lower air vent if the temperature is above 250 degrees or open up the lower air vent if the temperature drops below 255 degrees F and add few more hot coals.
- Check every hour if more water needs to add in the drip pan and add more hot coals using tongs along with another pouch of wood chips to keep the smoke going.
- Let smoke for 3 hours or until meat is cooked through and inserted meat thermometer register 160 degrees F temperature.
- Serve when ready.

Spicy Chicken Thighs

TOTAL COOK TIME 4 HOURS

Ingredients for 3 servings

- Chicken thighs – 6

The Rub

- Garlic powder – 1 tablespoon
- Salt – 1 tablespoon
- Ground black pepper – 2 tablespoon
- Red chili powder – 2 tablespoons
- Paprika – 2 tablespoons
- Cayenne pepper – 2 tablespoons
- Dried thyme – 1 tablespoon

The Fire

- Firstly, let soak 4 cups of wood chips, any flavor, in warm water for 30 minutes and then make packets of soaked woodchips, 1 cup per packet, by wrapping them in an aluminum foil.
- Arrange unlit charcoals on one side of charcoal grate into the smoker, then top with hot charcoals.
- Place a drip pan on the other side of smoker, 3/4 full with water and set smoking grate in place.
- Set the lid and wait until the temperature reached 225 degrees through temperature gauge or temperature probes while keeping more hot coals prepare.

METHOD

- In the meantime, brush olive oil all over chicken thighs.

- Stir together ingredients for rub and sprinkle generously on the chicken thighs.

- When ready to smoke, place a prepared pouch of woodchips over charcoal and when to start to smoke, brush the smoking grate with oil generously, place chicken thighs on the grate above the drip pan and insert thermometer probe in the thickest part of the meat.

- Set lid on smoker and monitor temperature through temperature gauge or temperature probes and maintain it.

- Close down the lower air vent if the temperature is above 250 degrees or open up the lower air vent if the temperature drops below 255 degrees F and add few more hot coals.

- Check every hour if more water needs to add in the drip pan and add more hot coals using tongs along with another pouch of wood chips to keep the smoke going.

- Let smoke for 4 hours, rotating halfway through, or until meat is cooked through and inserted meat thermometer register 150 to 165 degrees F temperature.

- Serve straightaway.

Maple Chipotle Chicken Breast

TOTAL COOK TIME 3 HOURS

INGREDIENTS FOR 4 SERVINGS

- Chicken breasts – 4

The Rub

- Onion powder – 1 teaspoon
- Garlic powder – 1 teaspoon
- Salt – 1 teaspoon
- Ground black pepper – 1/2 teaspoon
- Chipotle powder – 2 teaspoons
- Maple syrup, and more as needed for basting – 1/3 cup

The Fire

- Firstly, let soak 3 cups of wood chips, any flavor, in warm water for 30 minutes and then make packets of soaked woodchips, 1 cup per packet, by wrapping them in an aluminum foil.
- Arrange unlit charcoals on one side of charcoal grate into the smoker, then top with hot charcoals.
- Place a drip pan on the other side of smoker, 3/4 full with water and set smoking grate in place.
- Set the lid and wait until the temperature reached 225 degrees through temperature gauge or temperature probes while keeping more hot coals prepare.

METHOD

- In the meantime, season chicken breasts.

- For this, stir together all the ingredients for rub until combined, then coat each chicken breast with it by dipping and gently massage.

- When ready to smoke, place a prepared pouch of woodchips over charcoal and when to start to smoke, brush the smoking grate with oil generously, place chicken breasts on the grate above the drip pan and insert thermometer probe in the thickest part of the meat.

- Set lid on smoker and monitor temperature through temperature gauge or temperature probes and maintain it.

- Close down the lower air vent if the temperature is above 250 degrees or open up the lower air vent if the temperature drops below 255 degrees F and add few more hot coals.

- Check every hour if more water needs to add in the drip pan and add more hot coals using tongs along with another pouch of wood chips to keep the smoke going.

- Let smoke for 3 hours, basting with maple syrup every hour, or until meat is cooked through and inserted meat thermometer register 165 degrees F temperature.

- Serve straightaway.

Chicken Wings

TOTAL COOK TIME 3 HOURS

INGREDIENTS FOR 4 SERVINGS

- Chicken wings – 6 pounds

THE RUB

- Onion powder – 1 teaspoon
- Garlic powder – 1 teaspoon
- Salt – 1 teaspoon
- Ground black pepper – 3 teaspoons
- Red chili powder – 2 tablespoons
- Cayenne pepper – 1 teaspoon
- Smoked paprika – 2 tablespoons
- Ground cumin – 1 teaspoon
- Olive oil – 2 tablespoon

THE FIRE

- Firstly, let soak 3 cups of wood chips, any flavor, in warm water for 30 minutes and then make packets of soaked woodchips, 1 cup per packet, by wrapping them in an aluminum foil.
- Arrange unlit charcoals on one side of charcoal grate into the smoker, then top with hot charcoals.
- Place a drip pan on the other side of smoker, 3/4 full with water and set smoking grate in place.
- Set the lid and wait until the temperature reached 225 degrees through temperature gauge or temperature probes while keeping more hot coals prepare.

METHOD

- Before setting smoker, marinate chicken wings.

- For this, stir together all the ingredients for rub until combined and place in a large container.

- Add chicken wings, toss to coat and let marinate for 1 hour.

- When ready to smoke, place a prepared pouch of woodchips over charcoal and when to start to smoke, brush the smoking grate with oil generously, place chicken wings on the grate above the drip pan and insert thermometer probe in the thickest part of the meat.

- Set lid on smoker and monitor temperature through temperature gauge or temperature probes and maintain it.

- Close down the lower air vent if the temperature is above 250 degrees or open up the lower air vent if the temperature drops below 255 degrees F and add few more hot coals.

- Check every hour if more water needs to add in the drip pan and add more hot coals using tongs along with another pouch of wood chips to keep the smoke going.

- Let smoke for 2 hours and 30 minutes to 3 hours or until meat is cooked through and inserted meat thermometer register 165 degrees F temperature.

- Then transfer chicken wings to the other side of the grate, over the coals, and let smoke for 5 minutes per side until crispy.

- When done, remove chicken wings from the smoker and let rest for 5 minutes before serving.

CHICKEN HALVES

TOTAL COOK TIME 4 HOURS

INGREDIENTS FOR 5 SERVINGS

- Whole chicken – 1

THE BRINE

- Lemon, sliced – 1
- Salt – 1/2 cup
- Brown sugar – 3/4 cup
- Soy sauce – 1/4 cup
- Lemon juice – 1/2 cup
- Water – 3 quarts

THE RUB

- Hardcore Carnivore Red – 3 tablespoons
- Hardcore Carnivore Amplify – 2 tablespoon

THE FIRE

- Firstly, let soak 3 cups of wood chips, any flavor, in warm water for 30 minutes and then make packets of soaked woodchips, 1 cup per packet, by wrapping them in an aluminum foil.
- Arrange unlit charcoals on one side of charcoal grate into the smoker, then top with hot charcoals.
- Place a drip pan on the other side of smoker, 3/4 full with water and set smoking grate in place.
- Set the lid and wait until the temperature reached 225 degrees through temperature gauge or temperature probes while keeping more hot coals prepare.

Method

- Before setting smoker, prepare chicken halves.
- Remove neck of a chicken and rinse the cavity until cleaned.
- Then make a cut along the breastbone of chicken using a pair of shear and divide chicken into two halves by making a cut on side of the spine, discard spine.
- Stir together ingredients of brine in a large container until sugar dissolves, then add chicken halves and let soak in the refrigerator for overnight.
- Then rinse chicken thoroughly, pat dry and then sprinkle with seasonings.
- Let chicken halves rest for 30 minutes.
- When ready to smoke, place a prepared pouch of woodchips over charcoal and when to start to smoke, brush the smoking grate with oil generously, place chicken halves on the grate above the drip pan and insert thermometer probe in the thickest part of the meat.
- Set lid on smoker and monitor temperature through temperature gauge or temperature probes and maintain it.
- Close down the lower air vent if the temperature is above 250 degrees or open up the lower air vent if the temperature drops below 255 degrees F and add few more hot coals.
- Check every hour if more water needs to add in the drip pan and add more hot coals using tongs along with another pouch of wood chips to keep the smoke going.
- Let smoke for 3 hours or until meat is cooked through and inserted meat thermometer register 165 degrees F temperature.
- When done, remove chicken halves from smoker and wrap them loosely with an aluminum foil for 30 minutes.
- Serve straightaway.

CHAPTER-5 TURKEY RECIPES

Whole Turkey

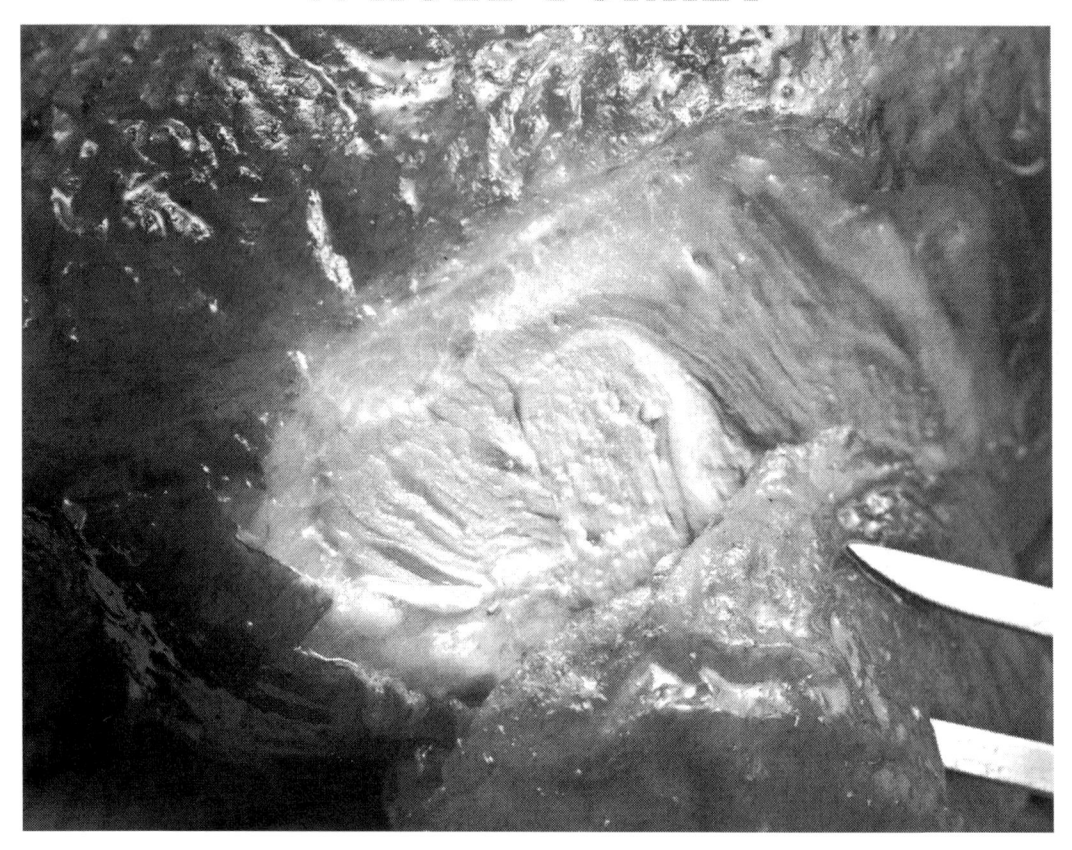

TOTAL COOK TIME 10 HOURS

INGREDIENTS FOR 12 SERVINGS

- Whole Turkey – 10 pounds

OTHER INGREDIENTS

- Apple, cored and quartered – 1
- White onion, peeled and quartered – 1
- Garlic powder – 1 tablespoon
- Minced garlic – 2 tablespoons
- Seasoned salt – 2 tablespoons
- Salt – 1 tablespoon
- Ground black pepper – 1 tablespoon
- Butter, unsalted – 1/2 cup
- Carbonated beverage, cola flavored – 24 ounces

THE FIRE

- Firstly, let soak 10 cups of wood chips, any flavor, in warm water for 30 minutes and then make packets of soaked woodchips, 1 cup per packet, by wrapping them in an aluminum foil.
- Arrange unlit charcoals on one side of charcoal grate into the smoker, then top with hot charcoals.
- Place a drip pan on the other side of smoker, 3/4 full with water and set smoking grate in place.
- Set the lid and wait until the temperature reached 225 degrees through temperature gauge or temperature probes while keeping more hot coals prepare.

METHOD

- In the meantime, prepare the turkey.

- For this, rinse turkey thoroughly, then pat dry and rub with garlic and sprinkle seasoned salt over the outside of turkey.

- Place the turkey in a roasting pan, fill its cavity with remaining ingredients and then loosely cover with aluminum foil.

- When ready to smoke, place a prepared pouch of woodchips over charcoal and when start to smoke, place the turkey in the roasting pan on the grate above the drip pan and insert thermometer probe in the thickest part of the meat.

- Set lid on smoker and monitor temperature through temperature gauge or temperature probes and maintain it.

- Close down the lower air vent if the temperature is above 250 degrees or open up the lower air vent if the temperature drops below 255 degrees F and add few more hot coals.

- Check every hour if more water needs to add in the drip pan and add more hot coals using tongs along with another pouch of wood chips to keep the smoke going.

- Let smoke for 10 hours, basting every hour with the juices in the roasting pan, or until meat is cooked through and inserted meat thermometer register 180 degrees F temperature.

- Serve when ready.

TURKEY BREAST

TOTAL COOK TIME 4 HOURS

INGREDIENTS FOR 6 SERVINGS

- Turkey breast, skinless – 1

TURKEY LEGS

TOTAL COOK TIME 4 HOURS

INGREDIENTS FOR 10 SERVINGS

- Turkey legs – 10

THE BRINE

- Onion powder – 3 tablespoons
- Garlic powder – 3 tablespoons
- Salt – 1 cup

- Ground black pepper – 1 1/2 tablespoons
- Brown sugar – ½ cup
- Paprika – 1 tablespoon
- Ground cloves – 1 teaspoon
- Ground allspice – 1 teaspoon
- Dried thyme – 3 tablespoons
- Dried sage – 3 tablespoons
- Liquid smoke – 1 teaspoon
- Water – 16 cups

THE FIRE

- Firstly, let soak 4 cups of wood chips, any flavor, in warm water for 30 minutes and then make packets of soaked woodchips, 1 cup per packet, by wrapping them in an aluminum foil.
- Arrange unlit charcoals on one side of charcoal grate into the smoker, then top with hot charcoals.
- Place a drip pan on the other side of smoker, 3/4 full with water and set smoking grate in place.
- Set the lid and wait until the temperature reached 300 degrees through temperature gauge or temperature probes while keeping more hot coals prepare.

METHOD

- Before setting smoker, prepare turkey legs.
- For this, place all the ingredients for the brine in a large pot and stir until combined.

- Place the pot over medium-high heat and bring to boil.

- Then remove the pot from heat and let cool completely.

- In the meantime, rinse turkey legs, pat dry and divide evenly between two large containers.

- Cover with cooled brine and let soak in the refrigerator for overnight.

- When ready to smoke, place a prepared pouch of woodchips over charcoal and when start to smoke, brush the smoking grate with oil generously

- Remove turkey legs from brine, then place on the grate above the drip pan and insert thermometer probe in the thickest part of the meat.

- Set lid on smoker and monitor temperature through temperature gauge or temperature probes and maintain it.

- Close down the lower air vent if the temperature is above 325 degrees or open up the lower air vent if the temperature drops below 300 degrees F and add few more hot coals.

- Check every hour if more water needs to add in the drip pan and add more hot coals using tongs along with another pouch of wood chips to keep the smoke going.

- Let smoke for 4 hours or until meat is cooked through and nicely browned on all sides.

- Serve immediately.

TURKEY WINGS

TOTAL COOK TIME 2 HOURS

INGREDIENTS FOR 4 SERVINGS

- Turkey wings, tip removed – 4

The Rub

- garlic powder – 1 teaspoon
- salt – 1 teaspoon
- white sugar – 1 tablespoon
- Red chili powder – 3 tablespoons
- cayenne pepper – 1/2 teaspoon

The Rub

- Limes – 2

The Fire

- Firstly, let soak 2 cups of wood chips, any flavor, in warm water for 30 minutes and then make packets of soaked woodchips, 1 cup per packet, by wrapping them in an aluminum foil.
- Arrange unlit charcoals on one side of charcoal grate into the smoker, then top with hot charcoals.
- Place a drip pan on the other side of smoker, 3/4 full with water and set smoking grate in place.
- Set the lid and wait until the temperature reached 275 degrees through temperature gauge or temperature probes while keeping more hot coals prepare.

METHOD

- In the meantime, prepare turkey wings.

- For this, stir together ingredients for turkey wings in a large bowl until combined.

- Then add turkey wings and toss to coat.

- When ready to smoke, place a prepared pouch of woodchips over charcoal and when start to smoke, brush the smoking grate with oil generously, place seasoned turkey wings on the grate above the drip pan and insert thermometer probe in the thickest part of the meat.

- Set lid on smoker and monitor temperature through temperature gauge or temperature probes and maintain it.

- Close down the lower air vent if the temperature is above 300 degrees or open up the lower air vent if the temperature drops below 275 degrees F and add few more hot coals.

- Check every hour if more water needs to add in the drip pan and add more hot coals using tongs along with another pouch of wood chips to keep the smoke going.

- Let smoke for 2 hours or until meat is cooked through and inserted meat thermometer register 170 degrees F temperature.

- Drizzle lime juice over turkey wings and serve.

BACON-WRAPPED TURKEY BREAST

TOTAL COOK TIME 4 HOURS

INGREDIENTS FOR 8 SERVINGS

- Turkey breasts – 7 pounds
- Slices of bacon – 12

THE BRINE

- Cranberry juice – 4 cups
- Sugar – 1/2 cup
- Coarse salt – 1/4 cup
- Sprigs of rosemary – 4
- Sprigs of thyme – 4
- Head of garlic, peeled and smashed – 1

THE FIRE

- Firstly, let soak 2 cups of wood chips, any flavor, in warm water for 30 minutes and then make packets of soaked woodchips, 1 cup per packet, by wrapping them in an aluminum foil.
- Arrange unlit charcoals on one side of charcoal grate into the smoker, then top with hot charcoals.
- Place a drip pan on the other side of smoker, 3/4 full with water and set smoking grate in place.
- Set the lid and wait until the temperature reached 225 degrees through temperature gauge or temperature probes while keeping more hot coals prepare.

Method

- Before setting smoker, prepare turkey breasts.
- For this, place all the ingredients for the brine in a large pot and stir until sugar dissolves completely.
- Add turkey breasts, cover pot and let soak for overnight in the refrigerator.
- Then rinse turkey breasts thoroughly, pat dry and wrap with turkey slices.
- When ready to smoke, place a prepared pouch of woodchips over charcoal and when start to smoke, brush the smoking grate with oil generously, place wrapped turkey breasts on the grate above the drip pan and insert thermometer probe in the thickest part of the meat.
- Set lid on smoker and monitor temperature through temperature gauge or temperature probes and maintain it.
- Close down the lower air vent if the temperature is above 250 degrees or open up the lower air vent if the temperature drops below 255 degrees F and add few more hot coals.
- Check every hour if more water needs to add in the drip pan and add more hot coals using tongs along with another pouch of wood chips to keep the smoke going.
- Let smoke for 3 hours or until meat is cooked through and inserted meat thermometer register 160 degrees F temperature.
- When done, wrap turkey breast with aluminum foil loosely and let stand for 30 minutes at room temperature.
- Slice and serve.

CHAPTER-6 FISH RECIPES

BROWN SUGAR SMOKED SALMON

TOTAL COOK TIME 1 HOUR

INGREDIENTS FOR 6 SERVINGS

- Salmon – 2 pounds

The Rub

- salt – 1 teaspoon
- brown sugar – 2 tablespoons
- Ground black pepper – 1 teaspoon
- Dried dill – 1 teaspoon

The Fire

- Firstly, let soak 1 cup of wood chips, any flavor, in warm water for 30 minutes and then make packets of soaked woodchips by wrapping them in an aluminum foil.
- Arrange unlit charcoals on one side of charcoal grate into the smoker, then top with hot charcoals.
- Place a drip pan on the other side of smoker, 3/4 full with water and set smoking grate in place.
- Set the lid and wait until the temperature reached 275 degrees through temperature gauge or temperature probes while keeping more hot coals prepare.

METHOD

- Before setting smoker, marinate salmon.

- For this, stir together ingredients for rub and sprinkle generously all over the salmon.

- Then place salmon in a refrigerator and let marinate for 1 hour.

- When ready to smoke, place a prepared pouch of woodchips over charcoal and when start to smoke, brush the smoking grate with oil generously, place seasoned salmon on the grate above the drip pan and insert thermometer probe in the thickest part of the meat.

- Set lid on smoker and monitor temperature through temperature gauge or temperature probes and maintain it.

- Close down the lower air vent if the temperature is above 275 degrees or open up the lower air vent if the temperature drops below 250 degrees F and add few more hot coals.

- Let smoke for 1 hour or until meat is cooked through and inserted meat thermometer register 145 degrees F temperature.

- Serve straightaway.

Smoked Trout Dip

TOTAL COOK TIME 3 HOURS

Ingredients for 6 servings

- Trout fillets – 2 pounds

The Brine

- Salt – ¼ cup
- Water – 1 quart

The Dip

- Chopped parsley – 2 teaspoons
- Ground white pepper – 1 teaspoon
- Chopped fresh chives – 2 tablespoons
- Seafood seasoning – 2 teaspoons
- Lemon juice – 1/4 cup
- Mayonnaise – 1/2 cup
- Sour cream – 1/4 cup

The Fire

- Firstly, let soak 2 cups of wood chips, any flavor, in warm water for 30 minutes and then make packets of soaked woodchips, 1 cup per packet, by wrapping them in an aluminum foil.
- Arrange unlit charcoals on one side of charcoal grate into the smoker, then top with hot charcoals.
- Place a drip pan on the other side of smoker, 3/4 full with water and set smoking grate in place.
- Set the lid and wait until the temperature reached 160 degrees through temperature gauge or temperature probes while keeping more hot coals prepare.

METHOD

- Before setting smoker, prepare trout.

- For this, stir together ingredients for the brine in a large pot until salt dissolves completely.

- Add trout, then cover pot and let soak for 3 hours in the refrigerator.

- Then remove trout from brine, rinse thoroughly and pat dry completely.

- Place trout fillets in a sheet pan and let dry in the refrigerator for a day.

- When ready to smoke, place a prepared pouch of woodchips over charcoal and when start to smoke, brush the smoking grate with oil generously, place salmon fillets, skin side down, on the grate above the drip pan and insert thermometer probe in the thickest part of the meat.

- Set lid on smoker and monitor temperature through temperature gauge or temperature probes and maintain it.

- Close down the lower air vent if the temperature is above 250 degrees or open up the lower air vent if the temperature drops below 255 degrees F and add few more hot coals.

- Check every hour if more water needs to add in the drip pan and add more hot coals using tongs along with another pouch of wood chips to keep the smoke going.

- Let smoke for 3 hours or until fillets are cooked through and nicely browned on all sides.

- When done, remove fish fillet from smoker and let cool slightly.

- Then remove skin and flake the fillets.

- Add flaked trout into a bowl and add all the ingredients for the dip except for chives.

- Stir until well combined and garnish with chives.

- Spread over toasted crostini and serve.

SMOKED SARDINES

TOTAL COOK TIME 5 HOURS

INGREDIENTS FOR 5 SERVINGS

- Sardine, gutted – 20

THE BRINE

- Medium white onion, peeled and chopped – 1
- Chopped parsley – 1/2 cup
- Minced garlic – 1 tablespoon
- Salt – 1/4 cup
- Ground black pepper – 1 tablespoon
- Honey – 1/4 cup
- Water – 4 cups
- Bay leaves – 5

THE FIRE

- Firstly, let soak 5 cups of wood chips, any flavor, in warm water for 30 minutes and then make packets of soaked woodchips, 1 cup per packet, by wrapping them in an aluminum foil.
- Arrange unlit charcoals on one side of charcoal grate into the smoker, then top with hot charcoals.
- Place a drip pan on the other side of smoker, 3/4 full with water and set smoking grate in place.
- Set the lid and wait until the temperature reached 225 degrees through temperature gauge or temperature probes while keeping more hot coals prepare.

METHOD

- Before setting smoker, prepare sardine.
- Clean them, rinse thoroughly and pat dry.
- Place all the ingredients for the brine in a large pot and stir until salt dissolves completely.
- Place the pot over medium-high heat and bring the mixture to boil.
- Then remove the pot from heat and let cool completely.
- Add sardines, cover container and let soak for overnight in a container.
- Then remove sardine from the brine, rinse thoroughly, pat dry and dry completely in a cool place for 1 hour.
- When ready to smoke, place a prepared pouch of woodchips over charcoal and when start to smoke, brush the smoking grate with oil generously, place sardines on the grate above the drip.
- Set lid on smoker and monitor temperature through temperature gauge and maintain it.
- Close down the lower air vent if the temperature is above 250 degrees or open up the lower air vent if the temperature drops below 255 degrees F and add few more hot coals.
- Check every hour if more water needs to add in the drip pan and add more hot coals using tongs along with another pouch of wood chips to keep the smoke going.
- Let smoke for 5 hours or until meat is cooked through and inserted meat thermometer register 140 degrees F temperature.
- When done, cut their head off and serve with salad.

Caribbean Style Whole Red Snapper

TOTAL COOK TIME 1 HOUR

Ingredients for 4 servings

- Red snapper, scaled and cleaned – 4 pounds

The Rub

- Ginger, grated – 1/4 cup
- Minced garlic – 1 tablespoon
- Scotch bonnet pepper, cored and diced – 1

OTHER INGREDIENTS

- Red bell pepper, cored and julienned – 1
- Yellow bell pepper, cored and julienned – 1
- Cilantro – 1/4 cup
- White onion, peeled and julienned – 1
- Salt – 3 tablespoons
- Ground black pepper – 1 tablespoon
- Dark brown sugar – 2 tablespoon
- Lime juice – 1/4 cup
- Olive oil – 1/2 cup
- Coconut milk – 2 cups

THE FIRE

- Firstly, let soak 1 cup of wood chips, any flavor, in warm water for 30 minutes and then make packets of soaked woodchips by wrapping them in an aluminum foil.
- Arrange unlit charcoals on one side of charcoal grate into the smoker, then top with hot charcoals.
- Place a drip pan on the other side of smoker, 3/4 full with water and set smoking grate in place.
- Set the lid and wait until the temperature reached 225 degrees through temperature gauge or temperature probes while keeping more hot coals prepare.

METHOD

- Before setting smoker, prepare fish.

- For this, make 5 deep cut into the flesh of fish and season with salt and black pepper.

- Place onion, bell peppers and cilantro in a bowl and stir until mixed.

- Then place fish in a large baking dish and stuff with prepare onion-peppers mixture.

- Stir together ingredients for rub and rub generously all over the fish, with hands covered with gloves.

- Whisk together sugar, oil, lime juice and coconut milk until combined and pour this mixture over fish.

- Cover dish with plastic wrap and let marinate for 2 hours in the smoker, turning fish three times during this period.

- When ready to smoke, place a prepared pouch of woodchips over charcoal and when start to smoke, brush the smoking grate with oil generously.

- Remove fish from the marinade, then place it on the grate above the drip pan and insert thermometer probe in the thickest part of the meat.

- Set lid on smoker and monitor temperature through temperature gauge or temperature probes and maintain it.

- Close down the lower air vent if the temperature is above 250 degrees or open up the lower air vent if the temperature drops below 255 degrees F and add few more hot coals.

- Let smoke for 1 hour or until fish is cooked through and flesh is very tender.

CHAPTER-7 SEAFOOD RECIPES

CRAB LEGS

TOTAL COOK TIME 30 MINUTES

INGREDIENTS FOR 10 SERVINGS

- Crab legs – 10 pounds

The Sauce

- Dried Parsley – 1 Tablespoon
- Crab Boil seasoning – ½ teaspoon
- BBQ Rub – 2 Tablespoons
- Lemon, juiced – 1
- Butter, unsalted – 1 pound

The Fire

- Firstly, let soak 1 cup of wood chips, any flavor, in warm water for 30 minutes and then make packets of soaked woodchips by wrapping them in an aluminum foil.
- Arrange unlit charcoals on one side of charcoal grate into the smoker, then top with hot charcoals.
- Place a drip pan on the other side of smoker, 3/4 full with water and set smoking grate in place.
- Set the lid and wait until the temperature reached 225 degrees through temperature gauge or temperature probes.

METHOD

- In the meantime, prepare crab legs.
- For this, place a small saucepan over low heat, add butter and let heat until melt completely.
- Stir in remaining ingredients for the sauce until combined and transfer the sauce to a bowl.
- Working on one crab leg at a time, dredge it into sauce and reserve remaining sauce for basting legs during smoking.
- When ready to smoke, place a prepared pouch of woodchips over charcoal and when start to smoke, brush the smoking grate with oil generously, place dredged crab legs on the grate above the drip pan.
- Set lid on smoker and monitor temperature through temperature gauge or temperature probes and maintain it.
- Close down the lower air vent if the temperature is above 250 degrees or open up the lower air vent if the temperature drops below 255 degrees F and add few more hot coals.
- Let smoke for 30 minutes, basting with reserved sauce every 10 minutes, or cooked through.
- Serve crab legs with lemon wedges.

GARLIC PRAWNS

TOTAL COOK TIME 30 MINUTES

INGREDIENTS FOR 6 SERVINGS

- Large prawns – 24

THE RUB

- Onion powder – 1 teaspoon
- Garlic powder – 1 teaspoon
- Minced garlic – 1 ½ teaspoons
- Salt – 1 tablespoon
- Paprika – 2 teaspoons
- Brown sugar – ¼ cup

THE FIRE

- Firstly, let soak 1 cup of wood chips, any flavor, in warm water for 30 minutes and then make packets of soaked woodchips by wrapping them in an aluminum foil.
- Arrange unlit charcoals on one side of charcoal grate into the smoker, then top with hot charcoals.
- Place a drip pan on the other side of smoker, 3/4 full with water and set smoking grate in place.
- Set the lid and wait until the temperature reached 225 degrees through temperature gauge or temperature probes.

Method

- Before setting smoker, let prawns marinate.
- For this, stir together ingredients for rub except for minced garlic in a bowl and rub generously on prawns.
- Let rub with garlic and let marinate for 2 hours in the refrigerator.
- When ready to smoke, place a prepared pouch of woodchips over charcoal and when start to smoke, brush the smoking grate with oil generously, place marinated prawns on the grate above the drip pan.
- Set lid on smoker and monitor temperature through temperature gauge and maintain it.
- Close down the lower air vent if the temperature is above 250 degrees or open up the lower air vent if the temperature drops below 255 degrees F and add few more hot coals.
- Let smoke for 30 minutes or until prawns turn pink.
- Serve straightaway.

Smoked Baby Octopus

TOTAL COOK TIME 1 HOUR AND 30 MINUTES

INGREDIENTS FOR 8 SERVINGS

- Baby Octopus – 2 pounds

The Brine

- Small white onion, peeled and chopped – 1/2
- Minced garlic – 3 tablespoons
- Sea salt – 2 tablespoons
- Ground black pepper – 1 teaspoon
- Apple cider vinegar – 1 tablespoon
- Olive oil – 2 tablespoons
- Water – 1 quart
- Ice cubes – 2 cups

The Fire

- Firstly, let soak 2 cups of wood chips, any flavor, in warm water for 30 minutes and then make packets of soaked woodchips, 1 cup per packet, by wrapping them in an aluminum foil.
- Arrange unlit charcoals on one side of charcoal grate into the smoker, then top with hot charcoals.
- Place a drip pan on the other side of smoker, 3/4 full with water and set smoking grate in place.
- Set the lid and wait until the temperature reached 225 degrees through temperature gauge or temperature probes while keeping more hot coals prepare.

METHOD

- Before setting smoker, let octopus soak in brine.

- For this, stir together ingredients for the brine in a large container until salt is dissolved completely.

- Add octopus, then cover the container and let soak for overnight in the refrigerator.

- Then remove octopus from the brine, rinse thoroughly, pat dry and dry completely in cool place for 30 minutes.

- When ready to smoke, place a prepared pouch of woodchips over charcoal and when start to smoke, brush the smoking grate with oil generously, place octopus on the grate above the drip pan and insert thermometer probe in the thickest part of the meat.

- Set lid on smoker and monitor temperature through temperature gauge or temperature probes and maintain it.

- Close down the lower air vent if the temperature is above 250 degrees or open up the lower air vent if the temperature drops below 255 degrees F and add few more hot coals.

- Check every hour if more water needs to add in the drip pan and add more hot coals using tongs along with another pouch of wood chips to keep the smoke going.

- Let smoke for 1 hour and 30 minutes or until cooked through and nicely browned.

- Serve straightaway.

SMOKED OYSTERS

TOTAL COOK TIME 2 HOURS

INGREDIENTS FOR 6 SERVINGS

- Oysters, in the shell – 50

Other Ingredients

- White wine – 1 cup
- Olive oil – 1/4 cup
- Water – 1 cup

The Fire

- Firstly, let soak 2 cups of wood chips, any flavor, in warm water for 30 minutes and then make packets of soaked woodchips, 1 cup per packet, by wrapping them in an aluminum foil.
- Arrange unlit charcoals on one side of charcoal grate into the smoker, then top with hot charcoals.
- Place a drip pan on the other side of smoker, 3/4 full with water and set smoking grate in place.
- Set the lid and wait until the temperature reached 145 degrees through temperature gauge or temperature probes while keeping more hot coals prepare.

Method

- Before setting smoker, prepare oysters.
- For this, rinse oysters thoroughly.
- Stir together water and white wine in a large pot and bring broth to boil.
- Then remove the pot from heat and add oysters in a single layer.
- Cover pot and let steam for 2 to 3 minutes or until oysters are open.
- Transfer these oysters to a baking sheet and treat remaining oysters in the same manner.

- Then tie these oysters in a cheesecloth and remove debris by draining the cooking liquid completely.

- Remove oysters from shells using a sharp knife, place that muscle into the broth and let soak for 20 minutes.

- When ready to smoke, place a prepared pouch of woodchips over charcoal and when start to smoke, brush the smoking grate with oil generously, place oysters on the grate above the drip pan and insert thermometer probe in the thickest part of the meat.

- Set lid on smoker and monitor temperature through temperature gauge or temperature probes and maintain it.

- Close down the lower air vent if the temperature is above 150 degrees or open up the lower air vent if the temperature drops below 140 degrees F and add few more hot coals.

- Check every hour if more water needs to add in the drip pan and add more hot coals using tongs along with another pouch of wood chips to keep the smoke going.

- Let smoke for 2 hours or until cooked through.

- When done, transfer oysters to a bowl, drizzle with oil and toss to coat.

- Serve straightaway.

CHAPTER-8 GAME & RABBIT RECIPES

SMOKED DUCK

TOTAL COOK TIME 4 HOURS

INGREDIENTS FOR 2 SERVINGS

- Large duck – 1

THE RUB

- Salt – as needed
- Maple syrup – 1/4 cup

THE FIRE

- Firstly, let soak 4 cups of wood chips, any flavor, in warm water for 30 minutes and then make packets of soaked woodchips, 1 cup per packet, by wrapping them in an aluminum foil.
- Arrange unlit charcoals on one side of charcoal grate into the smoker, then top with hot charcoals.
- Place a drip pan on the other side of smoker, 3/4 full with water and set smoking grate in place.
- Set the lid and wait until the temperature reached 225 degrees through temperature gauge or temperature probes while keeping more hot coals prepare.

METHOD

- In the meantime, prepare duck.
- For this, clean the cavity of duck, rinse thoroughly and pat dry.
- Then season cavity with salt generously and brush maple syrup over the outside of duck.
- When ready to smoke, place a prepared pouch of woodchips over charcoal and when start to smoke, brush the smoking grate with oil generously, place duck on the grate above the drip pan and insert thermometer probe in the thickest part of the meat.
- Set lid on smoker and monitor temperature through temperature gauge or temperature probes and maintain it.

- Close down the lower air vent if the temperature is above 250 degrees or open up the lower air vent if the temperature drops below 255 degrees F and add few more hot coals.

- Check every hour if more water needs to add in the drip pan and add more hot coals using tongs along with another pouch of wood chips to keep the smoke going.

- Let smoke for 4 hours, basting with maple syrup every hour, or until meat is cooked through and inserted meat thermometer register 150 to 165 degrees F temperature.

- When done, let duck cool completely and then slice to serve.

Smoked Pheasant

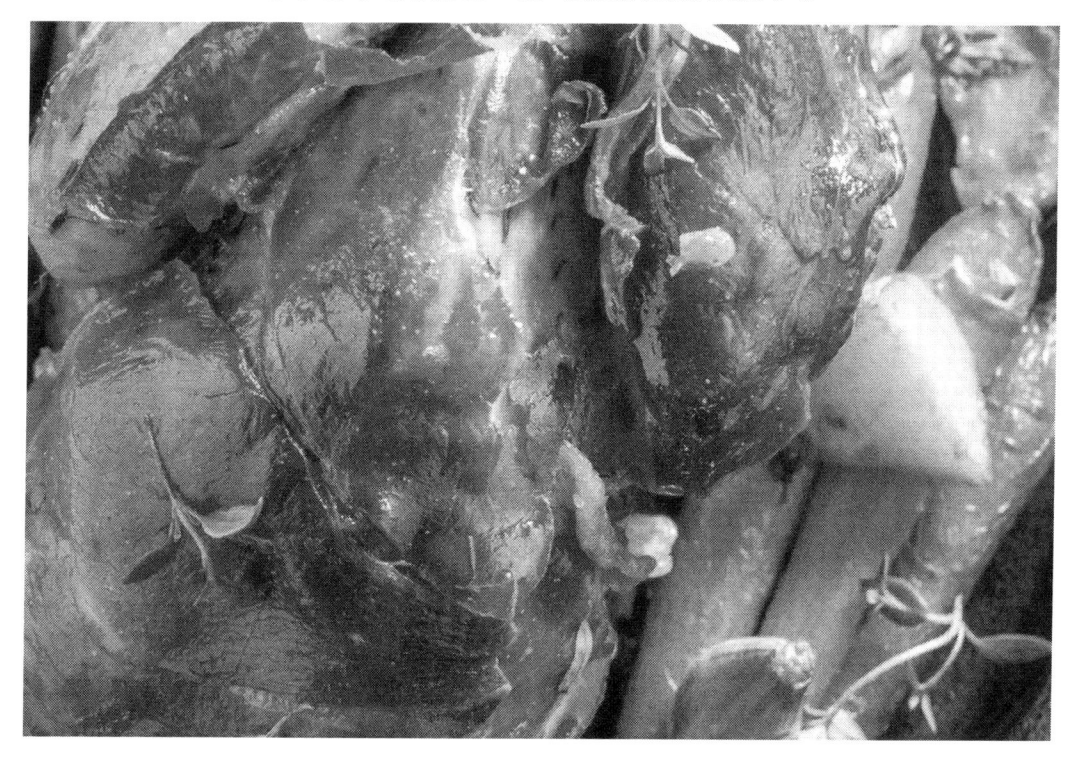

TOTAL COOK TIME 5 HOURS

Ingredients for 2 servings

- Whole pheasants – 2

The Brine

- Salt – 1/4 cup
- Brown sugar – 1/4 cup
- Water – 4 cups

The Baste

- Maple syrup – 2 cups

The Fire

- Firstly, let soak 5 cups of wood chips, any flavor, in warm water for 30 minutes and then make packets of soaked woodchips, 1 cup per packet, by wrapping them in an aluminum foil.
- Arrange unlit charcoals on one side of charcoal grate into the smoker, then top with hot charcoals.
- Place a drip pan on the other side of smoker, 3/4 full with water and set smoking grate in place.
- Set the lid and wait until the temperature reached 225 degrees through temperature gauge or temperature probes while keeping more hot coals prepare.

Method

- Before setting smoker, let pheasant soak in brine.
- For this, stir together ingredients for broth in a large container until salt and sugar are dissolved completely.
- Add pheasants, cover container and let soak for 12 hours in the refrigerator.
- Then remove pheasants from brine, pat dry and dry completely in a cool place for 3 hours.
- When ready to smoke, place a prepared pouch of woodchips over charcoal and when start to smoke, brush the smoking grate with oil generously, place pheasants on the grate above the drip pan and insert thermometer probe in the thickest part of the meat.

- Set lid on smoker and monitor temperature through temperature gauge or temperature probes and maintain it.

- Close down the lower air vent if the temperature is above 250 degrees or open up the lower air vent if the temperature drops below 255 degrees F and add few more hot coals.

- Check every hour if more water needs to add in the drip pan and add more hot coals using tongs along with another pouch of wood chips to keep the smoke going.

- Let smoke for 3 to 5 hours, brushing with maple syrup every hour or until meat is cooked through and inserted meat thermometer register 160 degrees F temperature.

- When done, remove pheasants from the smoker, then brush again with maple syrup and let rest for 20 minutes before serving.

Citrus Goose Breast

TOTAL COOK TIME 4 HOURS

Ingredients for 8 servings

- Goose breast halves – 8

The Marinade

- Dried minced onion – 1 tablespoon
- Garlic powder – 1 teaspoon
- Brown sugar – 1/3 cup
- Soy sauce – 1/4 cup
- Honey – 1/4 cup
- Yellow mustard – 1/3 cup
- Orange juice – 1/2 cup
- Olive oil – 1/3 cup

The Fire

- Firstly, let soak 4 cups of wood chips, any flavor, in warm water for 30 minutes and then make packets of soaked woodchips, 1 cup per packet, by wrapping them in an aluminum foil.
- Arrange unlit charcoals on one side of charcoal grate into the smoker, then top with hot charcoals.
- Place a drip pan on the other side of smoker, 3/4 full with water and set smoking grate in place.
- Set the lid and wait until the temperature reached 30 degrees through temperature gauge or temperature probes while keeping more hot coals prepare.

METHOD

- Before setting smoker, let goose breasts marinate.

- For this, stir together all the ingredients for the goose in a large bowl until combined.

- Add goose, toss to coat, then cover bowl and let marinate for 6 hours in the refrigerator.

- When ready to smoke, place a prepared pouch of woodchips over charcoal and when start to smoke, brush the smoking grate with oil generously, place marinated goose breasts on the grate above the drip pan and insert thermometer probe in the thickest part of the meat, reserve marinade.

- Set lid on smoker and monitor temperature through temperature gauge or temperature probes and maintain it.

- Close down the lower air vent if the temperature is above 250 degrees or open up the lower air vent if the temperature drops below 255 degrees F and add few more hot coals.

- Check every hour if more water needs to add in the drip pan and add more hot coals using tongs along with another pouch of wood chips to keep the smoke going.

- Let smoke for 3 to 4 hours, brushing with marinade every hour, or until meat is cooked through and inserted meat thermometer register 165 degrees F temperature.

- Slice and serve.

BUFFALO CHUCK ROAST

TOTAL COOK TIME 6 HOURS

Ingredients for 6 servings

- Buffalo chuck roast – 3 pounds

The Rub

- Onion powder – 1/2 teaspoon
- Garlic powder – 1 teaspoon
- Salt – 1 1/2 teaspoon
- Ground black pepper – 1 teaspoon
- Smoked paprika – 1 teaspoon
- Worcestershire sauce – 2 tablespoons

The Fire

- Firstly, let soak 6 cups of wood chips, any flavor, in warm water for 30 minutes and then make packets of soaked woodchips, 1 cup per packet, by wrapping them in an aluminum foil.
- Arrange unlit charcoals on one side of charcoal grate into the smoker, then top with hot charcoals.
- Place a drip pan on the other side of smoker, 3/4 full with water and set smoking grate in place.
- Set the lid and wait until the temperature reached 225 degrees through temperature gauge or temperature probes while keeping more hot coals prepare.

Method

- In the meantime, prepare the roast.
- For this, first massage roast with Worcestershire sauce.
- Stir together remaining ingredients for rub until mixed and then rub generously all over the beef.
- When ready to smoke, place a prepared pouch of woodchips over charcoal and when start to smoke, brush the smoking grate with oil generously, place seasoned beef chuck roast on the grate above the drip pan and insert thermometer probe in the thickest part of the meat.
- Set lid on smoker and monitor temperature through temperature gauge or temperature probes and maintain it.
- Close down the lower air vent if the temperature is above 250 degrees or open up the lower air vent if the temperature drops below 255 degrees F and add few more hot coals.
- Check every hour if more water needs to add in the drip pan and add more hot coals using tongs along with another pouch of wood chips to keep the smoke going.
- Let smoke for 5 to 6 hours or until meat is cooked through and inserted meat thermometer register temperature between 130 to 140 degrees F.
- When done, wrap the roast in aluminum foil loosely and let rest for 20 minutes.
- Then slice and serve.

Bacon Wrapped Rabbit

TOTAL COOK TIME 2 HOURS

Ingredients for 4 servings

- Whole rabbit, skinned – 1

The Brine

- Salt – ¼ cup
- Brown sugar – 1/3 cup
- Water – 8 cups

Other ingredients

- BBQ sauce – as needed
- Bacon slices – 14

The Fire

- Firstly, let soak 2 cups of wood chips, any flavor, in warm water for 30 minutes and then make packets of soaked woodchips, 1 cup per packet, by wrapping them in an aluminum foil.

- Arrange unlit charcoals on one side of charcoal grate into the smoker, then top with hot charcoals.

- Place a drip pan on the other side of smoker, 3/4 full with water and set smoking grate in place.

- Set the lid and wait until the temperature reached 225 degrees through temperature gauge or temperature probes while keeping more hot coals prepare.

Method

- Before setting smoker, let rabbit soak into the brine.

- For this, stir together ingredients of brine in a large container until sugar and salt dissolved completely.

- Add rabbit, cover container and let soak for 1 day in the refrigerator.

- Then remove rabbit from brine, rinse thoroughly, pat dry and completely dry in a cool place for 3 hours.

- Brush rabbit with BBQ sauce and then wrap with bacon slices and secure slices with toothpicks.

- When ready to smoke, place a prepared pouch of woodchips over charcoal and when to start to smoke, brush the smoking grate with oil generously, place wrapped rabbit on the grate above the drip pan and insert thermometer probe in the thickest part of the meat.

- Set lid on smoker and monitor temperature through temperature gauge or temperature probes and maintain it.

- Close down the lower air vent if the temperature is above 250 degrees or open up the lower air vent if the temperature drops below 255 degrees F and add few more hot coals.

- Check every hour if more water needs to add in the drip pan and add more hot coals using tongs along with another pouch of wood chips to keep the smoke going.

- Let smoke for 2 hours or until meat is cooked through and inserted meat thermometer register 165 degrees F temperature.

- Serve when ready.

CHAPTER-9 VEGETABLES & SNACK RECIPES

Smoke-Roasted Root Vegetables

TOTAL COOK TIME 1 HOUR

INGREDIENTS FOR 4 SERVINGS

The Vegetables

- Large carrots – 2
- Medium-size potatoes – 2
- Medium-size sweet potatoes – 2

The Spice Mix

- Sea salt – 1 ½ teaspoon
- Ground black pepper – 1 teaspoon
- Olive oil – 1/4 cup, and more for drizzling

Other Ingredients

- Chopped parsley – 2 tablespoons

The Fire

- Firstly, let soak 1 cup of wood chips, any flavor, in warm water for 30 minutes and then make packets of soaked woodchips, 1 cup per packet, by wrapping them in an aluminum foil.

- Arrange unlit charcoals on one side of charcoal grate into the smoker, then top with hot charcoals.

- Place a drip pan on the other side of smoker, 3/4 full with water and set smoking grate in place.

- Set the lid and wait until the temperature reached 350 degrees through temperature gauge.

METHOD

- In the meantime, prepare vegetables.
- For this, do not peel vegetables and sliced into 2-inch pieces.
- Place these vegetables in a large bowl, add ingredients for spice mix and toss to coat.
- Transfer these vegetables into an aluminum tray, about 8 by 12 inch.
- When ready to smoke, place a prepared pouch of woodchips over charcoal and when start to smoke, place aluminum tray containing vegetables on the grate above the drip pan.
- Set lid on smoker and monitor temperature through temperature gauge or temperature probes and maintain it.
- Let smoke for 1 hour or until vegetables are very tender.
- When done, drizzle oil over vegetables, then garnish with parsley and serve.

Smoked Corn On The Cob

TOTAL COOK TIME 1 HOUR

Ingredients for 6 servings

The Vegetable

- Ears of corn, with husk – 6
- Green onions, thinly sliced – 3

THE SAUCE

- Melted butter, unsalted – ¼ cup
- Brown sugar – 1 tablespoon
- Paprika – 1 teaspoon
- Onion powder – 1 teaspoon
- Garlic powder – ½ teaspoon
- Salt – ½ teaspoon

THE FIRE

- Firstly, let soak 1 cup of wood chips, any flavor, in warm water for 30 minutes and then make packets of soaked woodchips, 1 cup per packet, by wrapping them in an aluminum foil.
- Arrange unlit charcoals on one side of charcoal grate into the smoker, then top with hot charcoals.
- Place a drip pan on the other side of smoker, 3/4 full with water and set smoking grate in place.
- Set the lid and wait until the temperature reached 225 degrees through temperature gauge or temperature probes.

METHOD

- Before setting smoker, prepare corn.
- For this, remove back husk from corn by pulling it away and then remove silks.
- Fill a large pot half full with water, add ears of corn and pour in more water if corns are covered with water completely.
- Let corn soak for 4 hours, then drain them, pat dry completely using paper towels and gently pull back husk over corn.
- Stir together ingredients for sauce in a bowl until well combined.
- Brush this sauce generously over corns and sprinkle with green onions.
- When ready to smoke, place a prepared pouch of woodchips over charcoal and when start to smoke, add ears of corn on the grate above the drip pan.
- Set lid on smoker and monitor temperature through temperature gauge or temperature probes and maintain it.
- Close down the lower air vent if the temperature is above 250 degrees or open up the lower air vent if the temperature drops below 255 degrees F and add few more hot coals.
- Let smoke for 1 hour, corns halfway through, or until cooked through.
- When done, remove corns from smokers, let rest for 10 minutes and serve.

Smoked Artichokes

TOTAL COOK TIME 2 HOURS

Ingredients for 3 servings

The Vegetable

- Whole artichoke hearts, canned – 15

The Seasoning

- Cajun seasoning – 1 tablespoon
- Cayenne pepper – 1 tablespoon

The Fire

- Firstly, let soak 2 cups of wood chips, any flavor, in warm water for 30 minutes and then make packets of soaked woodchips, 1 cup per packet, by wrapping them in an aluminum foil.

- Arrange unlit charcoals on one side of charcoal grate into the smoker, then top with hot charcoals.

- Place a drip pan on the other side of smoker, 3/4 full with water and set smoking grate in place.

- Set the lid and wait until the temperature reached 225 degrees through temperature gauge or temperature probes while keeping more hot coals prepare.

Method

- In the meantime, prepare artichoke hearts.

- For this, cut each artichoke heart into halve.

- Stir together ingredients for seasoning and sprinkle generously all over artichoke hearts.

- When ready to smoke, place a prepared pouch of woodchips over charcoal and when start to smoke, brush the smoking grate with oil generously, place seasoned artichoke hearts on the grate above the drip pan.

- Set lid on smoker and monitor temperature through temperature gauge or temperature probes and maintain it.

- Close down the lower air vent if the temperature is above 250 degrees or open up the lower air vent if the temperature drops below 255 degrees F and add few more hot coals.

- Check every hour if more water needs to add in the drip pan and add more hot coals using tongs along with another pouch of wood chips to keep the smoke going.

- Let smoke for 2 hours or until artichoke hearts are cooked through and tender.

- Serve with herb mayonnaise and pork steaks.

Smoked Tomatillo Salsa

TOTAL COOK TIME 1 HOUR AND 30 MINUTES

INGREDIENTS FOR 6 SERVINGS

THE VEGETABLE

- Tomatillos – 6

The Seasoning

- Salt – 1 teaspoon
- Ground black pepper – ¾ teaspoon

The Salsa

- Chopped cilantro – ¼ cup
- Salt – 1 teaspoon
- Ground black pepper – 1 teaspoon
- Apple cider vinegar – 1/3 cup
- Water – 3 tablespoons

The Fire

- Firstly, let soak 2 cups of wood chips, any flavor, in warm water for 30 minutes and then make packets of soaked woodchips, 1 cup per packet, by wrapping them in an aluminum foil.
- Arrange unlit charcoals on one side of charcoal grate into the smoker, then top with hot charcoals.
- Place a drip pan on the other side of smoker, 3/4 full with water and set smoking grate in place.
- Set the lid and wait until the temperature reached 275 degrees through temperature gauge or temperature probes while keeping more hot coals prepare.

METHOD

- In the meantime, prepare tomatillos.

- For this, remove casing of tomatillos, then cut into quarters and then place in a sheet pan.

- Sprinkle with salt and black pepper and toss to coat.

- When ready to smoke, place a prepared pouch of woodchips over charcoal and when start to smoke, brush the smoking grate with oil generously, place sheet pan containing tomatillos on the grate above the drip pan.

- Set lid on smoker and monitor temperature through temperature gauge or temperature probes and maintain it.

- Close down the lower air vent if the temperature is above 250 degrees or open up the lower air vent if the temperature drops below 255 degrees F and add few more hot coals.

- Check every hour if more water needs to add in the drip pan and add more hot coals using tongs along with another pouch of wood chips to keep the smoke going.

- Let smoke for 1 hour and 30 minutes or until tender and roasted.

- When done, remove sheet pan from the smoker and transfer tomatillos into a blender.

- Add ingredients for salsa and pulse for 2 to 3 minutes at high speed or until smooth.

- Serve salsa with meats.

Smoked Jalapeño Poppers

TOTAL COOK TIME 1 HOUR AND 45 MINUTES

INGREDIENTS FOR 5 SERVINGS

THE VEGETABLE

- Medium jalapeno peppers, halved lengthwise – 10

OTHER INGREDIENTS

- Slices of bacon, thick cut – 4
- Grated cheddar cheese – 1 cup
- Cream cheese, softened – 4 ounces

THE FIRE

- Firstly, let soak 2 cups of wood chips, any flavor, in warm water for 30 minutes and then make packets of soaked woodchips, 1 cup per packet, by wrapping them in an aluminum foil.
- Arrange unlit charcoals on one side of charcoal grate into the smoker, then top with hot charcoals.
- Place a drip pan on the other side of smoker, 3/4 full with water and set smoking grate in place.
- Set the lid and wait until the temperature reached 250 degrees through temperature gauge or temperature probes while keeping more hot coals prepare.

Method

- Place a prepared pouch of woodchips over charcoal and when start to smoke, place slices of bacon on the grate above the drip pan.
- Close down the lower air vent if the temperature is above 250 degrees or open up the lower air vent if the temperature drops below 255 degrees F and add few more hot coals.
- Let smoke for 1 hour or until crispy.
- In the meantime, cut each jalapeno pepper in half and remove its seeds and ribs.
- Arrange these pepper halves on a sheet tray in a single layer and set aside until required.
- When bacon is done, chop it finely and transfer to a bowl.
- Add cheeses and stir until well mixed.
- Stuff this mixture into jalapeno peppers, about 1 tablespoon per pepper and then place a sheet pan on the smoker.
- Let smoke for 30 to 45 minutes or until cheese melt completely and peppers are slightly roasted.
- Serve straightaway.

Beef Jerky

TOTAL COOK TIME 4 HOURS

Ingredients for 6 servings

The Meat

- Beef roast – 2 pounds

The Marinade

- Jalapeno peppers, cored and sliced – 2
- Onion powder – 1 teaspoon
- Garlic powder – 1 teaspoon
- Salt – 1 tablespoon
- Ground black pepper – 2 teaspoons
- Dr. Pepper – 2 cups
- Worcestershire sauce – 1 tablespoon

The Fire

- Firstly, let soak 3 cups of wood chips, any flavor, in warm water for 30 minutes and then make packets of soaked woodchips, 1 cup per packet, by wrapping them in an aluminum foil.
- Arrange unlit charcoals on one side of charcoal grate into the smoker, then top with hot charcoals.
- Place a drip pan on the other side of smoker, 3/4 full with water and set smoking grate in place.
- Set the lid and wait until the temperature reached 170 degrees through temperature gauge or temperature probes while keeping more hot coals prepare.

Method

- Before setting smoker, marinade beef.
- For this, slice beef thinly against the grain and place in a large plastic bag.

- Place all the ingredients for marinade in a saucepan, stir until combined and bring to boil.

- Then reduce heat to low and let simmer for 15 minutes or more until sauce is reduced by half.

- Then remove the pan from heat and let cool completely.

- Add this cooled marinade to the beef, seal the bag and turn upside down until well coated.

- Place this bag in the refrigerator and let beef marinade for 12 hours.

- Then remove beef slices from marinade, pat dry using paper towels and place on jerky or cooling rack.

- When ready to smoke, place a prepared pouch of woodchips over charcoal and when smoke starts, place jerky rack on the smoker.

- Set lid on smoker and monitor temperature through temperature gauge or temperature probes and maintain it.

- Close down the lower air vent if the temperature is above 250 degrees or open up the lower air vent if the temperature drops below 255 degrees F and add few more hot coals.

- Check every hour if more water needs to add in the drip pan and add more hot coals using tongs along with another pouch of wood chips to keep the smoke going.

- Let smoke for 3 hours or until jerky is dry evenly and not soft.

- When done, transfer jerky immediately to a plastic bag and let steam for 30 minutes, don't seal the bag.

- Serve straightaway.

CHAPTER-10 SMOKING MEAT

SELECTING A SMOKER

You need to invest in a good smoker if you are going to smoke meat on a regular basis. Consider these options when buying a smoker. Here are two natural fire option for you:

- Charcoal smokers are fueled by a combination of charcoal and wood. Charcoal burns easily and the temperature remains steady, so you won't have any problem with a charcoal smoker. The wood gives a great flavor to the meat and you will enjoy smoking meats.

- Wood smoker: The wood smoker will give your brisket and ribs the best smoky flavor and taste, but it is a bit harder to cook with wood. Both hardwood blocks and chips are used as fuel.

CHOOSE YOUR WOOD

You need to choose your wood carefully because the type of wood you will use affect greatly to the flavor and taste of the meat. Here are a few options for you:

- Maple: Maple has a smoky and sweet taste and goes well with pork or poultry

- Alder: Alder is sweet and light. Perfect for poultry and fish.

- Apple: Apple has a mild and sweet flavor. Goes well with pork, fish, and poultry.

- Oak: Oak is great for slow cooking. Ideal for game, pork, beef, and lamb.

- Mesquite: Mesquite has a smoky flavor and extremely strong. Goes well with pork or beef.

- Hickory: Has a smoky and strong flavor. Goes well with beef and lamb.

- Cherry Has a mild and sweet flavor. Great for pork, beef, and turkey

THE RIGHT TEMPERATURE

- Start at 250F (120C): Start your smoker a bit hot. This extra heat gets the smoking process going.

- Temperature drop: Once you add the meat to the smoker, the temperature will drop, which is fine.

- Maintain the temperature. Monitor and maintain the temperature. Keep the temperature steady during the smoking process.

Avoid peeking every now and then. Smoke and heat two most important element make your meat taste great. If you open the cover every now and then you lose both of them and your meat loses flavor. Only the lid only when you truly need it.

DIFFERENCE BETWEEN COLD AND HOT SMOKING

Depending on the type of grill that you are using, you might be able to get the option to go for a Hot Smoking Method or a Cold Smoking One. The primary fact about these three different cooking techniques which you should keep in mind are as follows:

- **Hot Smoking:** In this technique, the food will use both the heat on your grill and the smoke to prepare your food. This method is most suitable for items such as chicken, lamb, brisket etc.
- **Cold Smoking:** In this method, you are going to smoke your meat at a very low temperature such as 30 degree Celsius, making sure that it doesn't come into the direct contact with the heat. This is mostly used as a means to preserve meat and extend their life on the shelf.
- **Roasting Smoke:** This is also known as Smoke Baking. This process is essentially a combined form of both roasting and baking and can be performed in any type of smoker with a capacity of reaching temperatures above 82 degree Celsius.

THE BASIC PREPARATIONS

- Always be prepared to spend the whole day and take as much time as possible to smoke your meat for maximum effect.
- Make sure to obtain the perfect Ribs/Meat for the meal which you are trying to smoke. Do a little bit of research if you need.
- I have already added a list of woods in this book, consult to that list and choose the perfect wood for your meal.
- Make sure to prepare the marinade for each of the meals properly. A great deal of the flavor comes from the rubbing.
- Keep a meat thermometer handy to get the internal temperature when needed.
- Use mittens or tongs to keep yourself safe
- Refrain yourself from using charcoal infused alongside starter fluid as it might bring a very unpleasant odor to your food
- Always make sure to start off with a small amount of wood and keep adding them as you cook.
- Don't be afraid to experiment with different types of wood for newer flavor and experiences.
- Always keep a notebook near you and note jot down whatever you are doing or learning and use them during the future session. This will help you to evolve and move forward.

THE CORE ELEMENTS OF SMOKING

Smoking is a very indirect method of cooking that relies on a number of different factors to give you the most perfectly cooked meal that you are looking for. Each of these components is very important to the whole process as they all work together to create the meal of your dreams.

- **Time**: Unlike grilling or even Barbequing, smoking takes a really long time and requires a whole lot of patience. It takes time for the smoky flavor to slowly get infused into the meats. Jus to bring things into comparison, it takes an about 8 minutes to fully cook a steak through direct heating, while smoking (indirect heating) will take around 35-40 minutes.
- **Temperature:** When it comes to smoking, the temperature is affected by a lot of different factors that are not only limited to the wind, cold air temperatures but also the cooking wood's dryness. Some smokers work best with large fires that are controlled by the draw of a chimney and restricted airflow through the various vents of the cooking chamber and firebox. While other smokers tend to require smaller fire with fewer coals as well as a completely different combination of the vent and draw controls. However, most smokers are designed to work at temperatures as low as 180 degrees Fahrenheit to as high as 300 degrees Fahrenheit. But the recommend temperature usually falls between 250 degrees Fahrenheit and 275 degrees Fahrenheit.
- **Airflow:** The level of air to which the fire is exposed to greatly determines how your fire will burn and how quickly it will burn the fuel. For instance, if you restrict air flow into the firebox by closing up the available vents, then the fire will burn at a low temperature and vice versa. Typically in smokers, after lighting up the fire, the vents are opened to allow for maximum airflow and is then adjusted throughout the cooking process to make sure that optimum flame is achieved.
- **Insulation:** Insulation is also very important when it comes to smokers as it helps to easily manage the cooking process throughout the whole cooking session. A good insulation allows smokers to efficiently reach the desired temperature instead of waiting for hours upon hours!

CONCLUSION

The book includes smoked meat recipes comprising beef, fish, seafood, pork, poultry, vegetables, and game. If you want to just treat yourself to mouthwatering, perfectly cooked smoked meat or entertain family or friends, this book will provide everything you need.

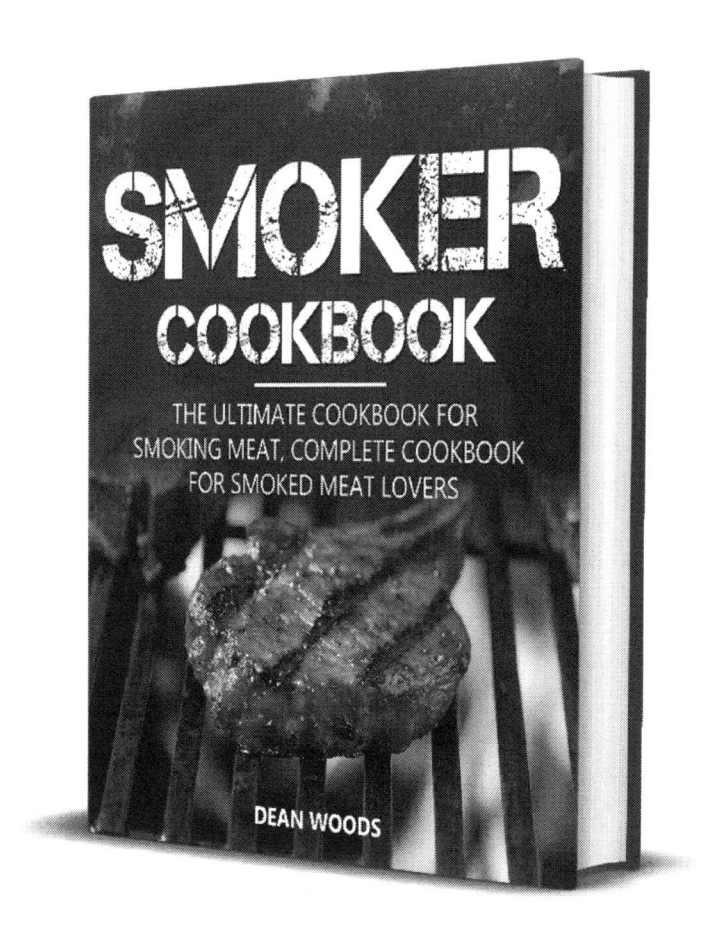

MY BOOKS

https://www.amazon.com/dp/1701878879

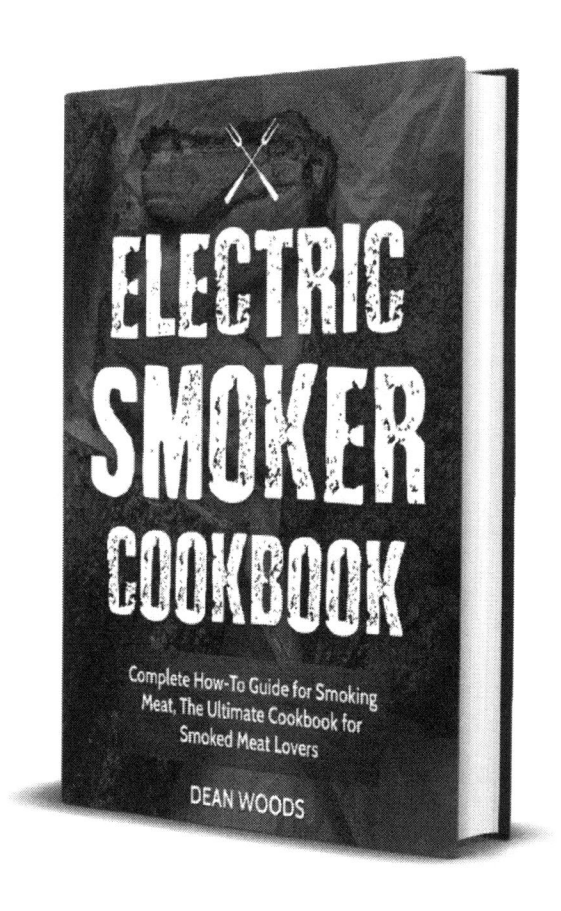

https://www.amazon.com/dp/1725606178

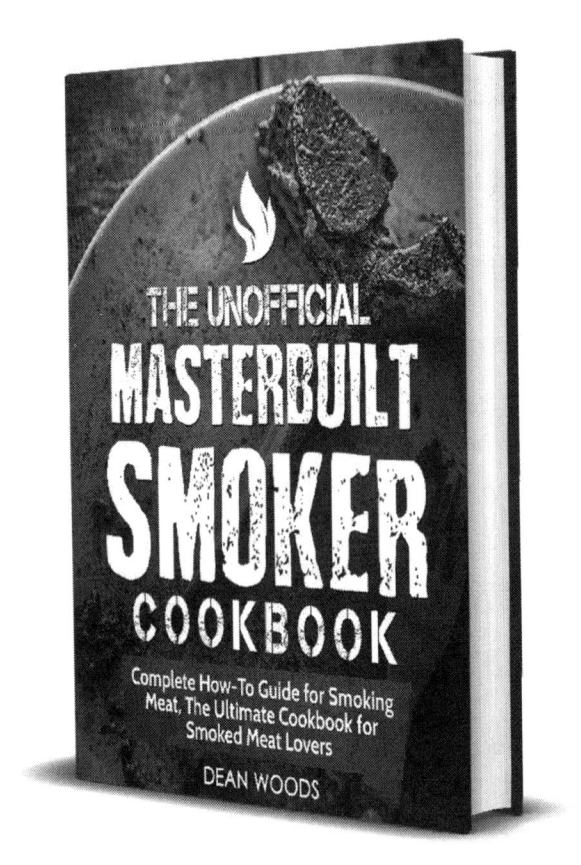

https://www.amazon.com/dp/1730758053

GET YOUR FREE GIFT

Subscribe to our Mail List and get your FREE copy of the book

'Smoking Meat: The Best 20 Recipes of Smoked Meat, Unique Recipes for Unique BBQ'

https://tiny.cc/smoke20

SMOKER COOKBOOK

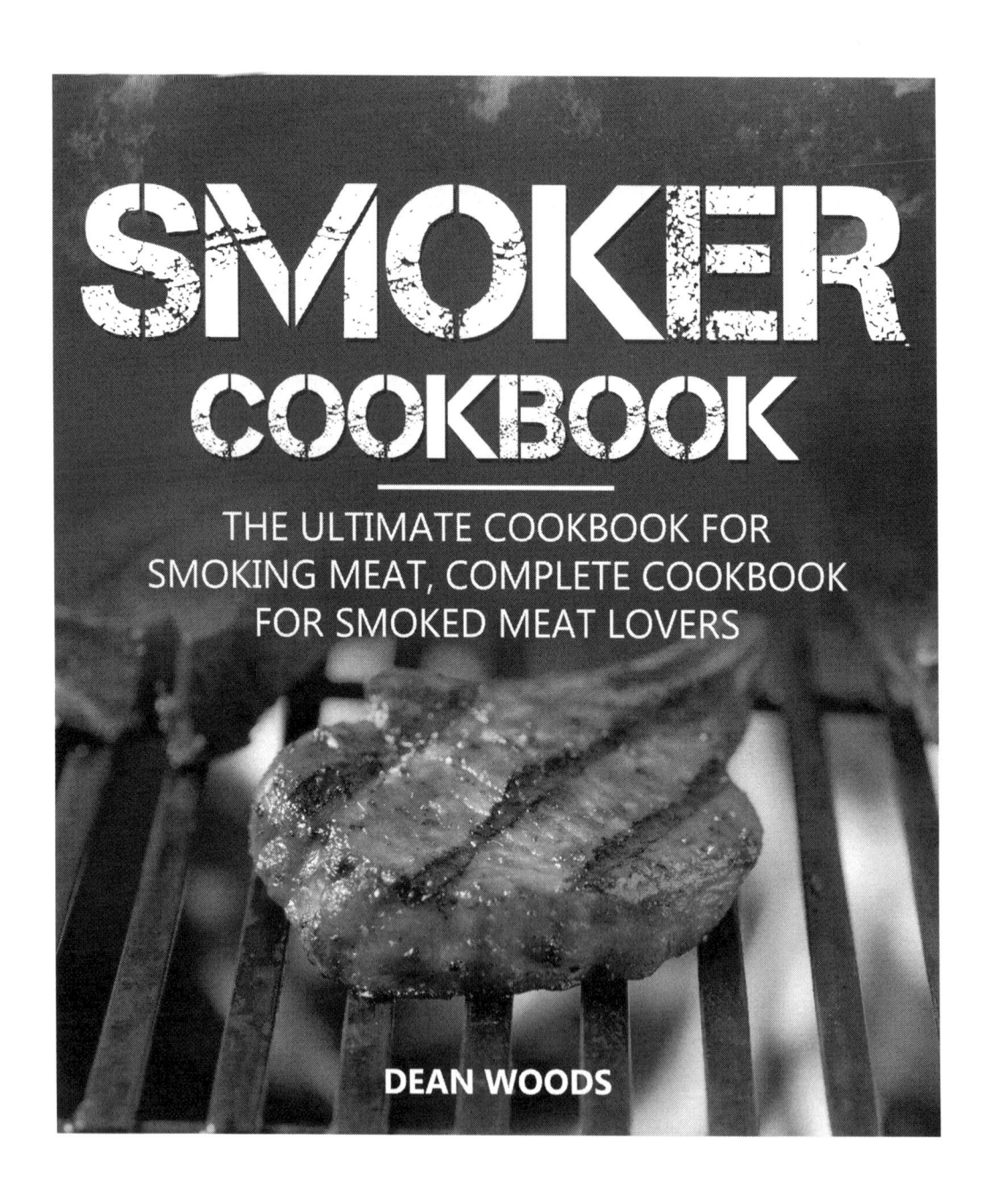

THE ULTIMATE COOKBOOK FOR SMOKING MEAT, COMPLETE COOKBOOK FOR SMOKED MEAT LOVERS

DEAN WOODS

Copyright 2020© Dean Woods

All rights reserved. No part of this guide may be reproduced in any form without permission in writing from the publisher except in the case of brief quotations embodied in critical articles or reviews.

Legal & Disclaimer: The information contained in this book and its contents is not designed to replace or take the place of any form of medical or professional advice; and is not meant to replace the need for independent medical, financial, legal or other professional advice or services, as may be required. The content and information in this book have been provided for educational and entertainment purposes only.

The content and information contained in this book have been compiled from sources deemed reliable, and it is accurate to the best of the Author's knowledge, information, and belief. However, the Author cannot guarantee its accuracy and validity and cannot be held liable for any errors and/or omissions. Further, changes are periodically made to this book as and when needed. Where appropriate and/or necessary, you must consult a professional (including but not limited to your doctor, attorney, financial advisor or such other professional advisor) before using any of the suggested remedies, techniques, or information in this book.

Upon using the contents and information contained in this book, you agree to hold harmless the Author from and against any damages, costs, and expenses, including any legal fees potentially resulting from the application of any of the information provided by this book.

This disclaimer applies to any loss, damages or injury caused by the use and application, whether directly or indirectly, of any advice or information presented, whether for breach of contract, tort, negligence, personal injury, criminal intent, or under any other cause of action.

You agree to accept all risks of using the information presented in this book.

You agree that by continuing to read this book, where appropriate and/or necessary, you shall consult a professional (including but not limited to your doctor, attorney, or financial advisor or such other advisor as needed) before using any of the suggested remedies, techniques, or information in this book.

Made in the USA
San Bernardino, CA
10 July 2020